Shanghai – the 'Pacesetter' of China's Reform and Opening Up

Zhou Zhenhua, et al., Eds

Published by
ACA Publishing Ltd.
University House
11-13 Lower Grosvenor Place
London SW1W 0EX, UK
Tel: +44 (0)20 7834 7676 Fax: +44 (0)20 7973 0076
E-mail: info@alaincharlesasia.com

Web: www.alaincharlesasia.com
Beijing Office
Tel: +86(0)10 8472 1250 Fax: +86(0)10 5885 0639
Written by Zhou Zhenhua etc.
Edited by David Lammie
Translated by Wang Xin
© People's Publishing House, 2015
This translation is published by ACA Publishing Ltd in association with
People's Publishing House

ALL RIGHTS RESERVED. NO PART OF THIS
PUBLICATION MAY BE REPRODUCED IN MATERIAL FORM,
BY ANY MEANS, WHETHER GRAPHIC,
ELECTRONIC, MECHANICAL OR OTHER, INCLUDING
PHOTOCOPYING OR INFORMATION STORAGE, IN
WHOLE OR IN PART, AND MAY NOT BE USED TO PREPARE
OTHER PUBLICATIONS WITHOUT WRITTEN
PERMISSION FROM THE PUBLISHER.

The greatest care has been taken to ensure accuracy but the publisher
can accept no responsibility for errors or omissions, or for any liability
occasioned by relying on its content.
ISBN 978-1-910760-14-7
Shanghai – the 'Pacesetter' of China's Reform and Opening Up is available
from the National Bibliographic Service of the British Library.

Preface

What is the state system of China? How has the Communist Party of China (CPC) managed to exercize long-term governance and to lead the Chinese people from one victory to another? What are the 'secrets' of the CPC's governance? What is China's development road? What significant strategies have been adopted in China? What is the next step in China's development? Why has China been able to achieve such rapid economic development? These are just some of the many questions frequently asked by the international community, especially foreign political parties and statesmen on their visits to China. For the purpose of providing answers to these questions and enabling readers to be informed about the real China and the CPC, we arranged for the *Understanding Modern China* Series (hereinafter referred to as the Series) to be written, to serve as elementary documents introducing the CPC, as well as China's development road, development theories and development experience.

The Series is inspired by the new philosophies, new ideas and new strategies for the country's governance put forward by General Secretary Xi Jinping since the 18th National Congress of the CPC, aimed at the following aspects: strenuously reflecting the development vision of 'the Chinese Dream' and the development prospects of the 'Two Centenary' goals; strenuously reflecting the coordinated promotion of the overall situation of a 'five-pronged approach to building socialism with Chinese characteristics to build up socialist economy, socialist democracy, socialist advanced culture, socialist harmonious society and socialist ecological civilisation; and the strategic arrangements for the 'Four-Pronged Comprehensive Strategy' comprehensively completing the building of a moderately prosperous society in all respects, comprehensively deepening reform in all respects, comprehensively advancing the rule of law, and comprehensively exercising strict discipline for the party; strenuously reflecting the 'new normal' facilitating and leading China's economic development and the implementation of the 'five major development concepts' to promote innovative, coordinated, green, open and shared development; strenuously reflecting the three major economic development strategies of the 'Belt and Road', the coordinated development of Beijing, Tianjin and Hebei province, and the Yangtze river economic belt. On the basis of a great number of fresh cases and experiences, the Series tells China's story, transmits China's voice, analyzes China's problems, and offers China solutions.

The Series has been written on the basis of telling China's story and transmitting China's voice, oriented around the following four aspects: the first is to illustrate the new measures taken to deepen reform since the 18th National Congress of the CPC, the new ideas on economic development and the new philosophy on foreign affairs, on the basis of an all-round introduction to the achievements since the reform and opening up; the second is to analyze the reason for the achievements, the underlying operating law, and the process of evolution, while presenting the development achievements of China's economy and society; the third is to keep to problem orientation and demand orientation, rather than attempt to be all-embracing and systematic, so as to clear up targeted doubts and confusion on the basis of the demands of foreign readers; the fourth is to introduce China not only in terms of 'where it is coming from', but also in terms of 'where it is going', for the purpose of enabling readers to know about China's historical development process on the one hand, and on the other hand, exemplifying and clarifying how China assures the organic unification of its past, present and future, the organic combination of legacy and innovation, and how China is planning its future development.

Under the guidance of the International Department of the CPC Central Committee, the writing of the Series has been organized by China Executive Leadership Academy Pudong (CELAP).

The International Department of the CPC Central Committee is the functional department of the CPC in charge of foreign affairs. So far, the CPC has established connections of various types with more than 600 political parties and organizations in over 160 countries and regions, which include left-wing and right-wing parties; both ruling parties and opposition parties. Foreign affairs work is of paramount importance to the CPC, and an indispensable component of national diplomacy as a whole, whose target is to promote state-to-state and people-to-people communication and understanding.

Preface

CELAP is a national leadership institution in China, and as a platform on which international cooperative training and exchange are carried out, CELAP has held fast to its characteristics of internationality and openness since March 2005 when it was founded. CELAP spares no effort in implementing international cooperative training, with target participants being foreign political parties and statesmen, high-ranking business executives and senior professionals. By the end of 2015, CELAP had offered training programs to more than 6,000 participants from over 130 countries, and thus has won wide recognition and received a favorable reception from the countries, regions and participants that are involved.

To cater for the needs of foreign participants, CELAP initiated the writing of the Series at the beginning of 2012, and after four years of modifications and improvements, the finalized manuscripts were completed at the end of 2015. The first batch of 10 books to be published in this Series are: *China's New Strategies for Governing the Country*; *The Communist Party of China: the Past, Present and Future of Party Building*; *China's Reform, Opening Up and Construction of Development Zones*; *The Framework of the Chinese Government and Public Services*; *A New Analysis of Urbanization in China*; *China's Agriculture and Rural Development in the Post-Reform Era*; *The Evolution of China's Diplomacy in the Modern Era*; *Leadership Selection and Appointment in China*; *Leadership Education and Training in China*; and *Shanghai – the 'Pacesetter' of China's Reform and Opening Up*.

The authors of the Series are mainly professionals in CELAP, and functionaries and specialists in the Development Research Center of the Shanghai Municipal People's Government, Shanghai Institute for International Studies and Hangzhou Research Center for Urban Studies.

The Series is published in Chinese and English, with the English translation done mainly by senior professors at Shanghai International Studies University, to whom thanks are due. Gratitude also goes to the People's Publishing House for its great support and positive suggestions in the process of writing and translating.

Writing such a series of textbooks for mature foreign students is a first in China. Constructive criticism is welcome, for the Series as a new endeavor can hardly be free from mistakes.

Editorial Committee of the *Understanding Modern China* Series
January 2016

The Editorial Committee of the Understanding Modern China Series

Directors: Guo Yezhou Feng Jun

Vice Directors: Zhou Zhongfei   An Yuejun

Members: (Listed alphabetically)

An Yuejun	Chen Zhong	Feng Jun
Guo Yezhou	He Lisheng	Jiang Haishan
Li Man	Li Yanhui	Liu Genfa
Liu Jingbei	Wang Guoping	Wang Jinding
Yang Jiemian	Zhao Shiming	Zheng Jinzhou
Zhou Zhenhua	Zhou Zhongfei	

Editor-in-Chief: Feng Jun

Alain Charles Asia (ACA) Publishing Ltd is delighted to be associated with the People's Publishing House to bring this series of 10 *Understanding Modern China* books to an English-speaking readership.

ACA, formerly known as ACP (Alain Charles Publishing) Ltd Beijing, was founded in October 1989 and was the first foreign-owned publishing company to be allowed to open an office in China.

In 2007, ACP Beijing was renamed ACA Publishing Ltd to better reflect its focus on China and the Asia-Pacific region. The company specialises in publishing books about China for international readers and has offices in Beijing and London.

ACA Publishing Ltd,

April 2016

Contents

Introduction X
   I. Teaching purpose X
   II. Structure and organization XI
   III. Focuses and challenges XII
   IV. Requirements XII

1. General Introduction to Shanghai 1
   I. A coastal city at the mouth of the Yangtze 1
   II. A modernized international metropolis developing from a small fishing village 2
   III. An immigrant city with a regional culture 3
   IV. A key city in the Asia-Pacific region rising again in the mid-phase of reform and opening up 5

2. The Development and Transformation of Shanghai's Economy ... 16
   I. Building the 'four centers' 16
   II. Forming an industrial structure focused on the service economy ... 20
   III. Reinforcing independent innovation capability and the construction of an innovative city 27
   IV. Reforming and developing the economic system with vitality ... 30
   V. Constantly improving the new pattern of an open economy 40

3. The Innovation of Shanghai's Social Administration 47
   I. Innovating the social administration pattern 47
   II. Actively developing community construction 56
   III. Establishing and perfecting the social security system 63
   IV. Developing and improving social undertakings 67
   V. Enhancing integrated population administration 70

4. The Development and Prosperity of Shanghai Culture 73
   I. Reforming and improving the cultural system mechanism 73

II.	Supporting the development of cultural creation industries 79
III.	Vigorously developing public cultural service 82
IV.	Prospering and developing urban tourism 86

5. The Protection and Renovation of Shanghai's Ecological Environment 94
    I. The rolling implementation of environmental protection and three-year action plans 94
    II. Implementing domain-oriented energy conservation and emission reduction 97
    III. Vigorously promoting the planning and building of an ecological green land system 101
    IV. Popularizing household garbage sorting and disposal 104
    V. Exploring the ecological architecture concept 106

6 The Operation and Administration of Shanghai City 110
    I. Exploring and promoting the devolution of the city administration focus 110
    II. Implementing a 'public transport priority' strategy 113
    III. Attaching great importance to food safety administration 115
    IV. Making and implementing plans to prevent and reduce disasters ...119
    V. Reinforcing the administration and maintenance of the urban appearance 121

7 The Development Prospects of Shanghai 124
    I. A global city with the capacity of global resource allocation 124
    II. Comprehensively deepening reform and improving the city administration system 127
    III. 'Innovation driving development, economic transformation being upgraded' 129
    IV. Constructing the main functional area and optimizing the spatial layout 132
    V. Fostering and developing strategic emerging industries 135
    VI. Building a cultural metropolis 138
    VII. Building a world-famous tourist city 141

Chapter Follow-up Questions and References 144

Introduction

In 1990, Deng Xiaoping, when speaking of the development and opening up of Pudong, said: "Shanghai is our trump card and it is a royal road for China's development and opening up." Since then, Shanghai has taken good advantage of the development and opening up of Pudong, properly dealing with the relationship between reform, development and stabilization, actively exploring a new mode of development that involves Chinese characteristics, the prevailing issues and the Shanghai character. As a result, the city has taken on a completely new look; industries have advanced by leaps and bounds; services supplied by government departments have been largely upgraded; people's living conditions have continuously improved; and its international status has been enhanced conspicuously. Today, Shanghai is integrating, with broader vision and accommodation, various forces into building socialism with Chinese characteristics, and Shanghai is continuing to play the role of a bellwether of reform and opening up, and the forerunner of scientific development, striving to help realize the China Dream of the great rejuvenation of the Chinese nation.

I. Teaching purpose

This textbook is designed to take the 30-year development of Shanghai after reform and opening up as the important background, and review and summarize the course of development, distinctive features, everyday events and future direction of Shanghai in aspects such as the reform and opening-up policy, economic construction, social construction, cultural construction and ecological civilization construction. The purpose is to tentatively reveal the development philosophy, development path and development experience of the super-large city of Shanghai, so that students have a deeper understanding of the China experience, China path and China philosophy, which may in turn help them to compare the Shanghai experience to practice in their own countries or regions.

II. Structure and organization

This textbook is composed of seven chapters. The first chapter illustrates, from both the horizontal and vertical perspectives, the natural, historical, cultural and social characteristics of Shanghai's development, its status in the country and in the world, and its development before and after reform and opening up as the leading city in the Yangtze River Delta and the Yangtze River Basin.

The second chapter focuses on some significant issues in the economic field, with a stress put on the target, the idea and path of the development and transformation of Shanghai's economy, the establishment and improvement of the market system, and the reform of the government itself.

The third chapter concentrates on some issues in the field of social administration, with an emphasis on the Shanghai mode in social administration, and its development and innovation in community construction, social security, social undertaking and integrated population management.

The fourth chapter focuses on issues in the cultural arena, particularly on the target, idea and path of Shanghai's cultural construction, as well as the development of the cultural industry, public cultural services and urban tourism.

The fifth chapter, centering on major issues in the field of ecological environment and case studies, illustrates the target, idea and path of Shanghai's ecological environment construction, and the theory and practice of green development.

The sixth chapter looks at major issues in the field of city operation administration, and stresses the target, idea and path of Shanghai city operation administration, and grid management, operation of the 12345 hotline and cases of integrated law enforcement.

The seventh chapter looks at the future development of Shanghai against the backdrop of national strategy, the integration of the Yangtze River Delta and the development of Shanghai itself. It assesses the city's vision of building Shanghai into a global city with the capability to allocate global resources, and makes illustrations from the perspectives of development guideline, development layout and development priority.

III. Focuses and challenges

This textbook focuses on the achievements of and lessons from Shanghai's reform and opening up, enabling students to understand the background of some significant issues, the development idea and development path in the process of development and transformation of Shanghai's economy and society, and to help students understand how Shanghai managed to develop from a small fishing village into a socialist, modern and international metropolis.

The challenges lie in how to know clearly about the needs and interests of foreign students, and through careful analysis of the features and requirements of intercultural communication, and by using plain language and giving real examples, to describe what is happening in both the country and the city, and to relate the development course of Shanghai, providing practical teaching materials for foreign students so that they can learn, understand and practice.

IV. Requirements

This textbook has an open outlook in terms of teaching contents, teaching requirements, representations and organizations, and may be regarded as a walking textbook. Teachers who have an open teaching philosophy are best able to use this textbook. The contents reflect the most basic and elementary knowledge structure. Since it contains historic information, it cannot include the latest dynamic conditions of Shanghai's development. That is why teachers should keep seeking new information, absorb new knowledge and keep stimulating the interest of their students. Students should take the textbook as a focused center that is to be radiated to the whole of society, for it is designed to go beyond the classroom environment to help people improve their understanding of the development of Shanghai's economy and society.

Due to limited knowledge and experience, there may be some points that have been inadvertently overlooked, and we would be very pleased to embrace any suggestions for improvement. Those who contributed to the writing of this textbook are Zhou Zhenhua, Qian Zhi, Cheng Jian, Liang Shaolian, Shi Xiaochen and Kang Fanghua.

Chapter 1

General Introduction to Shanghai

Shanghai is a super-large city that has prospered as a consequence of its harbor and trade, an immigrant city that is absorbing and accommodating, and a dynamic city that inherits glory and embraces dreams. Shanghai was the economic center of far east in the early 20th century, when it was known as an 'adventurers' paradise' and 'Paris of the orient'. At the end of the 20th century, Shanghai's role changed from 'laggard' to 'leader' in the reform and opening up of China, and with great effort it has risen to become a key city in the Asia-Pacific region at the start of the 21st century. With a vision for the future, Shanghai is currently accelerating the building of 'four centers' (an international economic, financial, trade and shipping center) and the building of a socialist, modernized and international metropolis, with the target of becoming a global city of finance.

I. A coastal city at the mouth of the Yangtze

Shanghai is located at the western edge of the Pacific Ocean, and the east edge of the Eurasian continent (with a longitude of 120°52' E to 122°16' E, and from 30°42' N to 31°48 N'). When you fly from distant parts of the world to the west bank of the Pacific Ocean and the central part of mainland China's arc-shaped coastline, what comes into view is a riverside and coastal metropolis bristling with high-rise buildings, and that is Shanghai.

Shanghai is situated at the mouth of Yangtze river, which is the longest river in China and the third longest in the world. It is equipped with advanced airports, seaports, information hubs and convenient rail, road and water networks leading to all parts of China. Shanghai also has a vast economic hinterland.

Shanghai is situated in the lower reaches of the Yangtze River Delta, and its area keeps growing because of the silt deposited by the Yangtze. At the end of 2010, Shanghai's land area was 6340.5 km^2, accounting for 0.06% of China's territory.

By the end of 2012, Shanghai had 16 districts, one county, 108 towns, two villages, 98 sub-district offices, 3,914 neighborhood committees and 1,613 village committees. According to China's sixth demographic census, conducted at midnight on November 1, 2010, the permanent residential population of Shanghai was 23.0191m.

II. A modernized international metropolis developing from a small fishing village

Compared with other cities in China, Shanghai does not have a long history. Over 6,000 years ago, land was formed in Qingpu, Songjiang and Jinshan in west Shanghai, and then the area was inhabited. Over 2,000 years ago, with more and more people living in the area, Shanghai grew up into a fishing village in the lower reaches of the Wusong river. During the Tang and Song dynasties, Shanghai gradually developed into a bustling harbor, which formed the basis of a thriving business on which the city's prosperity was based. In the Qing dynasty, Shanghai had already become a very important harbor, and though it was only China's 12th largest city in terms of population, it had grown from a small fishing village into a harbor city with great prospects.

Column 1-1 The origin of 'Shanghai'

The name Shanghai was first coined in the Song dynasty, when Shanghai was a burgeoning trade port composed of 18 river mouths (also called '*pu*'), one of which was known as Shanghai Pu and along its west bank there was Shanghai town. In 1292, Shanghai's name changed from Shanghai town to Shanghai county, and hence this was the origin of 'Shanghai'. In 1928, Shanghai was known as the special city of Shanghai, and in 1931, it was directly named Shanghai city. In 1949, Shanghai was made a municipality directly under the central government, and in 1958, 10 counties in Jiangsu province including Jiading and Baoshan were included in the administration of Shanghai, which resulted in a 10-fold expansion of its land area.

After the founding of the New China, the functions of Shanghai experienced some changes, from a center of shipping, trade and finance to the key industrial base and commercial center of China. Since reform and opening up in the 1980s, with the dramatic development of China's economy, Shanghai's functions in terms of trade, shipping and finance have been restored. By 2020, Shanghai plans to build itself into an international center for finance, trade, shipping and the economy, and into a socialist, modernized and international metropolis.

III. An immigrant city with a regional culture

Shanghai is a typical immigrant city. When it started as a commercial port, the population was only a little more than 200,000, but this grew to more than 1m in 1900. In 1935, Shanghai was the sixth largest city in the world, behind London, New York, Tokyo, Berlin and Chicago.

More than 80% of Shanghai's population originally came from provinces such as Jiangsu, Zhejiang, Guangdong, Anhui, Shandong, Hubei, Fujian, Henan, Jiangxi and Hunan. Immigrants from different parts of China have brought into Shanghai different food and traditional opera styles, thus contributing to the cultural pluralism of the city. These immigrants are mostly young men, well informed and capable, ready to learn and compete. They keep close contact with their origins and usually bear the features of a diversified culture and combine tolerance with great vitality and creativity.

In the wake of the opening of Shanghai as a commercial port, British, American and French concessions were established, resulting in the settlement of the earliest group of colonists including soldiers, officials, merchants and missionaries. Germans, Portuguese, Spanish, Italians and Dutch followed, and in 1854 there were more than 250 foreigners in the city. Thereafter, with the development of Shanghai and the outbreak of the two world wars, more and more international immigrants arrived in Shanghai, and by 1942, there were as many as 150,000 international immigrants from nearly 40 countries.

Column 1-2 Shanghai's regional culture

Shanghai regional culture was formed and developed with the rising of the typical immigrant city of Shanghai, and it is rooted in Chinese traditional culture, merging the quintessence of regional cultures such as Wu-Yue and absorbing the cultural elements of some western countries. Shanghai's regional culture was formed in this way, bearing new and unique characteristics, with its essence being 'absorbing and accommodating, committed to excellence, enlightened and farsighted, modest and generous'.

Domestic and international immigrants brought in cultures rich in diversity, and such cultures influenced and integrated with the others, which contributed to the formation of new cultural patterns, which is the Shanghai regional culture of 'absorbing and accommodating'.

In terms of architecture, a unique 'world architecture exhibition' was formed, combining Chinese and western styles. In terms of the traditional Chinese opera, a 'great union' of Chinese operas was formed, incorporating Shanghai local opera of 'Shen Qu' (Hu opera), the national Beijing opera, the local operas of Yue and Huai, along with foreign drama and ballet. And in terms of musical culture, besides the local music with typical local characteristics, there is also symphonic, brass band and orchestral music.

> **Column 1-3 The 'world architecture exhibition' on Shanghai Bund**
>
> Shanghai Bund contains a variety of 52 tall buildings of different styles including the Gothic, Baroque and Roman style, the most famous of which include the Customs House building, the Peace hotel and the original HSBC building. Though designed by different architects and varied in style, these buildings are unified in harmony, forming a beautiful skyline along the west bank of the Huangpu river, enjoying the great reputation of the 'world architecture exhibition'.

Today, Shanghai continues to attract immigrants from both home and abroad. Domestic immigrants are attracted by the advanced manufacturing and rapid development of the modern service industry, as well as the favorable living conditions and educational resources. At the end of 2012, the number of permanent residents from other provinces totaled 9.535m, and these people are the main source of population growth in Shanghai and they make great contributions to the development of the city's society and economy.

With the rapid development of the economy, the optimization of the business environment, the improvement in educational levels, and the enforcement of a series of preferential policies, more and more talented people from overseas are attracted to Shanghai. In 2012, the number of foreigners permanently living in Shanghai and recorded in the census register was 174,200, accounting for one quarter of foreigners living in the whole country. These foreigners are mainly from Japan, the US, Korea, France, Germany, Canada, Singapore, Australia, the UK and Malaysia. In addition, the number of foreigners who visited Shanghai temporarily in 2012 totaled 4.731m, and it was predicted that by 2015, the number of international students in Shanghai would have reached 70,000. Domestic and foreign immigrants have brought with them a diversified culture that keeps enriching Shanghai's regional culture. These immigrants have also made the city more dynamic and vibrant, enhancing the development of the city.

IV. A key city in the Asia-Pacific region rising again in the mid-phase of reform and opening up

After the founding of the New China in 1949, the development of Shanghai can be divided into three phases, with each phase lasting for 30 years. The first phase is from 1949 to 1978, the second 1978 to 2008, and currently, Shanghai is passing through its third 30-year phase of development.

1. The development of Shanghai in the 30 years prior to reform and opening up: the most important industrial base and main commercial center in China

From 1949 to 1978, after the accomplishment of taking over and restoring the economy, Shanghai gradually got its economic construction and social development on track, and achieved development under a highly centralized planned economic system.

Shanghai's first five-year plan lasted from 1953 to 1957, and it witnessed the socialist transformation of agriculture, the handicraft industry and capitalist industry and commerce. Shanghai, as the most important industrial base in China, realized rapid development of industrial production, and set up the preliminary foundation of socialist industrialization. In the meantime, the People's Bank of China was established and settled in the capital of Beijing to build a unified national banking system, which resulted in the loss of Shanghai's status as the country's financial center. It was also no longer the trade center, as a result of the establishment of the planned economy, and thus became the largest supply distribution center of the country, and foreign trade was conducted under the unified control of the central government.

The 'Great Leap Forward' movement that happened between 1958 and 1960 had a big impact on the economy of Shanghai, and the 'Cultural Revolution' that happened between 1966 and 1976 caused even greater harm to the development of the city's economy and society.

During the 30 years from 1949 to 1978, despite various factors hindering its economic development and construction, Shanghai retained its light and heavy industry infrastructure, and built a commercial network that was predominantly either state owned of collectively owned. Shanghai was transformed from being a center of shipping, trade and finance to the nation's most important industrial base and major commercial center, and thus became a center of industry and commerce.

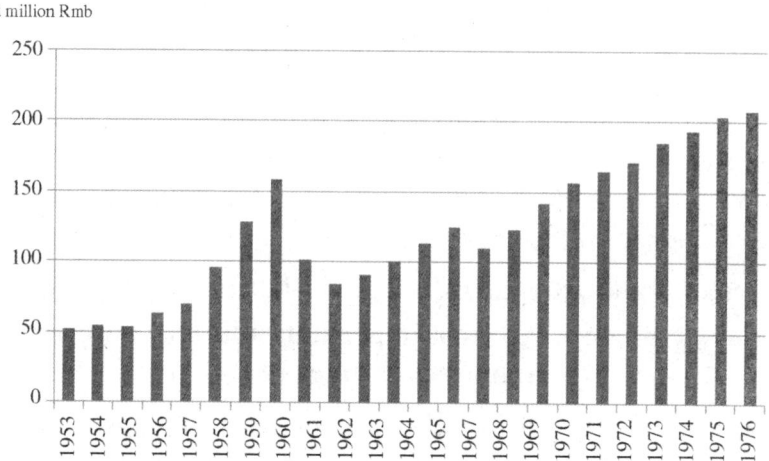

Figure 1-1 Shanghai's GDP growth from 1953 to 1976

2. The 30-year development of Shanghai after reform and opening up: rising once again as a key city in the Asia-Pacific region

Since 1978, with the introduction of the reform and opening-up policy, Shanghai's economy has developed rapidly and has risen to become a remarkable key city in the Asian-Pacific region.

The 1980s: the adjustment, reform and transformation of Shanghai

Since December 1978, Shanghai has concentrated on economic construction, with the economy developed in all aspects, the investment structure adjusted and city construction accelerated; Shanghai has reorganized its science and technology, culture, education and health, for the purpose of promoting development; Shanghai has implemented economic system reform and actively developed diverse areas of the economy; Shanghai has opened up to absorb foreign investment and introduce advanced technology.

– Reform of state-owned enterprises (SOEs) and the countryside. Shanghai, in the New China, is a region that has the most complete industrial system, the soundest planned system and the largest economy. Therefore, to carry out substantial reform, large numbers of SOEs must be revived. Shanghai started the reform process by 'delegating powers and benefits' and established various forms of economic responsibility systems by the organic combination of authority, responsibility and benefit, such as the practice of profit retention by enterprises, the implementation of 'replacement of profit by tax' and the reform of enterprise internal management, through which enterprises have gained more and more decision-making powers. Various types of production responsibility system were put into practice in the countryside, with the family contract responsibility system introduced in 1983 and land management on a larger scale in 1984.

– Making strategies of economic development. In 1984, Shanghai municipal government produced *Synopsis of the Report on the Strategy of Shanghai's Economic Development*, stating that Shanghai should fully exert its role as the key city with diversified functions in reform and opening up, implementing an opening up to the nation and to the world, accelerating the transformation of traditional industries, exploring emerging industries and developing the tertiary sector. The focus was laid upon developing trade, finance, consultancy services and tourism, and the employment of foreign capital was initiated and expanded.

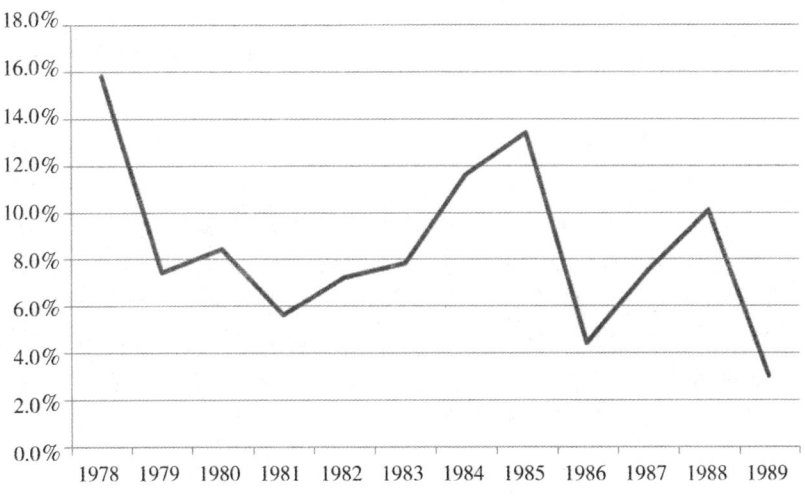

Figure 1-2 Shanghai's GDP growth from 1978 to 1989

– Introduction of foreign capital. In March 1985, Shanghai started the gradual utilization of foreign investment on a large scale. Foreign-owned enterprises in Shanghai are mainly owned by European, American and Japanese enterprises, which makes it different from Guangdong province whose foreign-owned enterprises are mainly owned by Hong Kong and Macau investors. In 1985, Shanghai ratified the establishment of 94 foreign-owned enterprises, attracting foreign capital of US$711m; the utilization of foreign capital and the introduction of technology between 1985 and 1987 was 2.5 times the total of foreign investment made prior to 1985. To optimize the environment for foreign capital development, Shanghai has also introduced various system innovations. Before 1988, owing to the low efficiency of administration, the ratification of a foreign investment project of US$1m required the examination of many government departments and more than 100 seals. To solve such a problem, Zhu Rongji, who was then mayor of Shanghai, decided to establish Shanghai Foreign Investment Working Committee, implementing a 'one-stop service' for foreign investment; as a result, foreign investors needed only one seal from Shanghai Foreign Investment Working Committee. This measure greatly simplified the ratification procedure of foreign investment, which played a key role in attracting foreign investment. In 1988, Shanghai Hongqiao Development Zone adopted international bidding for the paid transfer of land-use rights, and correspondingly issued more than 20 local regulations concerning foreign investment development, and such measures created a favorable environment for the development of Shanghai's foreign investment economy.

> **Column 1-4 Shanghai as a clustering place for transnational enterprises in China**
>
> Due to reform and opening up, Shanghai has forged closer connections with the world economy, and an increasingly sound environment for finance, shipping and services has made Shanghai a strategic node of transnational enterprises. More and more transnational companies have transferred their headquarters to Shanghai, making Shanghai a city with the highest concentration of transnational companies in the Chinese mainland. Up to the end of 2012, as many as 265 investment companies had settled in Shanghai, and 403 transnational companies had made their headquarters in the city.

– Building three development zones and developing an open economy. In the 1980s, Shanghai established three national level development zones in Puxi – Hongqiao, Minhang and Caohejing – and these development zones have become the highlights of the reform, opening up and development process. Of the three zones, Hongqiao development zone was then the only emerging commercial trade and commerce zone in China, characterized by foreign trade, and integrating exhibition, demonstration, office work, residence, catering and shopping.

Chapter 1

The 1990s: the resumption of Shanghai's internationalization

In 1990, China decided to explore and open up Pudong, practicing in Pudong the policy of creating economic and technological development zones (ETDZs) and special economic zones (SEZs). In 1992, the report of the 14th National Congress of the CPC stated: "The development and opening up of Shanghai Pudong shall be taken as the bellwether in order to further open up the cities along the Yangtze river. Shanghai will be established, as soon as possible, into an international economic, financial and trade center, driving the economic development of the Yangtze Delta and the whole Yangtze River Basin region." Shanghai's economy and city construction, therefore, developed at unprecedented speed.

- Accelerating reform. Shanghai has explored establishing the operating mechanism of a socialist market economy, and the economic system has been transformed from a planned economy to a socialist market economy. As a result, a series of factor markets such as capital, land, assets, labor force and technology have been developed. In addition, the real estate market has been established, the monetary market has been enlarged and the capital market has been expanded. What has been constructed is a market system involving securities, foreign exchange, shipping, inter-bank lending, futures, property rights, talent and technology, which takes the state-level market as the flagship, the regional market as the backbone and the local market as the base.

- Carrying forward opening up. Shanghai takes the development and opening up of Pudong as the flagship, aiming to build the city into an international center of economy, finance and trade, and to promote Shanghai's transformation from a traditional industrial city to international economic center. Significant adjustments have been made to its urban layout and industrial structure, and the city function has been changed from single manufacturing function to comprehensive service functions. Shanghai has established the priority to develop: city infrastructure, the tertiary industry and high and new technology, with the focus placed upon fast-developing industries such as finance and insurance, commerce and trade, transportation and communication, real estate, information consultancy and tourism. Shanghai will gradually phase out certain manufacturing industries such as textiles and nonferrous metallurgy, while supporting the six industrial pillar industries of automobiles, communication devices, power station equipment, steel, petrochemicals and household appliances. It will also foster high and new technology industries represented by the electronic information industry, modern biotechnology and medicine industry and new materials.

> **Column 1-5 The development and opening up of Pudong**
>
> Pudong is located on the east bank of the Huangpu river, and prior to its development, there was a huge disparity in the economic development of Pudong and Puxi. In 1990, Pudong accounted for only 8% of Shanghai's total economy, and the Lujiazui area was a mere shanty town composed of rudimentary houses. There was a widespread feeling among Shanghai citizens that they would prefer to have a one-bedroom apartment in Puxi than a house in Pudong, which show the huge gap between the two areas.
>
> On April 18, 1990, the central government officially proclaimed the development and opening up of Shanghai Pudong. Deng Xiaoping said: "The development of Pudong is of great significance, for this involves not only the development of Pudong but also that of Shanghai, and even the entire Yangtze River Delta and Yangtze River Basin area." The central government ratified the creation of national-level development zones with various functions in Pudong, such as Lujiazui finance and trade zone, Waigaoqiao Free Trade Zone, Jinqiao Export Processing Zone, Zhangjiang Hi-tech Park, Yangshan bonded port area and the comprehensive bonded zone of Pudong airport. The central government allocated a series of national-level major projects to Pudong which helped to deepen reform and expand opening up, with Pudong authorized to take the lead in carrying out a comprehensive supporting pilot reform. The gross regional product of Pudong New Area rose from Rmb6bn in 1990 to Rmb400.1bn in 2009, increasing 67-fold over 20 years, contributing nearly 30% of the Shanghai economy.

The 1990s witnessed Shanghai's most rapid development, and from 1990 to 1999 its GDP rose from Rmb75.645bn to Rmb403.496bn, increasing 5.3-fold, with an annual average increase of 20.5%. This was double the city's average increase in the 1980s, and more than 2% higher than the national average over the same period. The per capita GDP increased from Rmb5,818 in 1990 to Rmb30,805 in 1999; total industrial and agricultural output increased by 16.4% and 10.5% respectively; retail sales of consumer goods increased by an annual average of 18.06%; the per capita disposable income of urban families increased 19.6% annually, and that of rural families rose 16.4%.

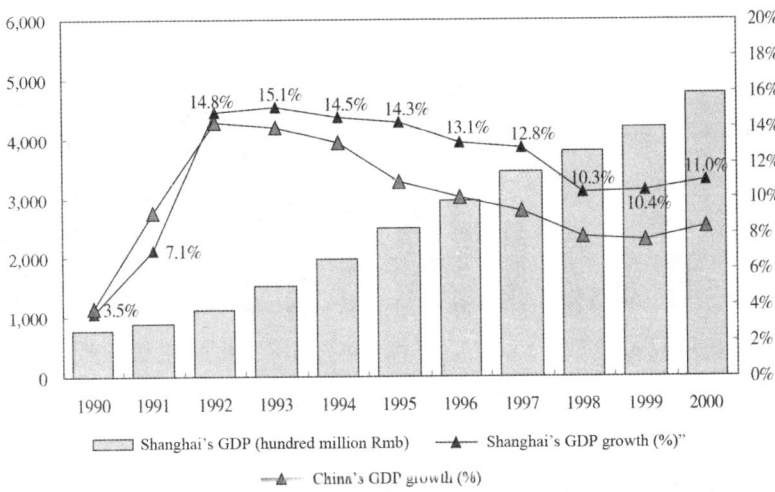

Figure 1-3 Economic growth in Shanghai and China in the 1990s

(3) From 2000 to 2008: Shanghai gradually emerges as a key city in the Asia-Pacific region

At the beginning of the 21st century, Shanghai's economy was confronted with a new development environment. First, China joined the World Trade Organization (WTO) at the end of 2001, laying an essential foundation for the integration of Shanghai's economy into the world. Second, Shanghai succeeded in bidding to host the 2010 World Exposition, which injected renewed vitality to the city's economic development. Third, China's economic development came to its periodical expansion stage, which acted as a great impetus to Shanghai's economy.

- Sustained and rapid economic development. Since 2000, Shanghai's economy has grown fast and steadily. From 2000 to 2012, its GDP rose from Rmb477.12bn to Rmb2.018172tn, a 4.2-fold increase; per capita GDP rose from US$3,630 to US$13,524, an increase of 3.7 times; local fiscal revenue rose from Rmb49.796bn to Rmb374.371bn, an increase of 7.5 times.

- A constantly optimized industrial structure. In the process of economic development, Shanghai has constantly adjusted and optimized its industrial structures; the urban industrial structure has become service industry oriented, with the tertiary industry developing rapidly and becoming more important. In 2011, the proportion between the primary, secondary and tertiary industries was 0.6:38.9:60.4, with the modern service industry playing an increasingly important role in the economy.

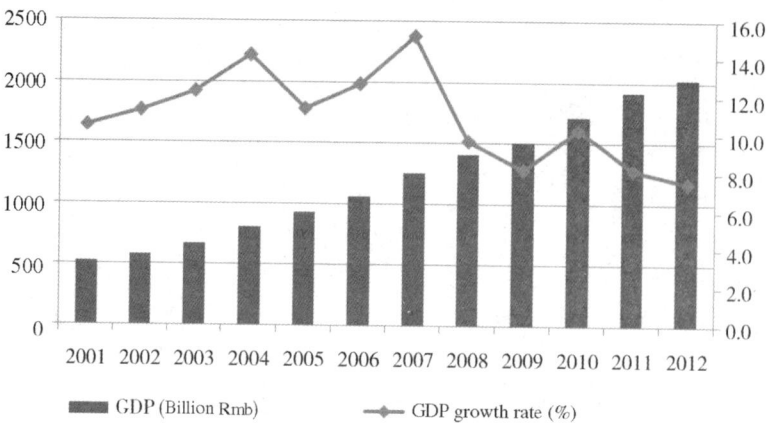

Figure 1-4 Shanghai's GDP growth between 2001 and 2012

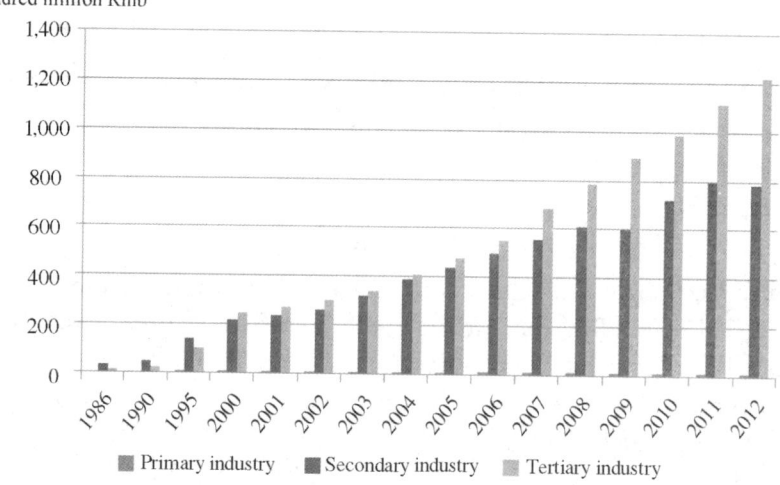

Figure 1-5 The added value structure of the three industries 1986-2012

Besides developing a modern service industry, Shanghai also attaches importance to the development of emerging high-tech industries. In 2012, Shanghai issued *The '12th Five-year Plan' of the Development of Emerging Strategic Industries in Shanghai,* with a focus placed upon such seven strategic emerging industries: new-generation information technology, high-end equipment manufacturing, biotechnology, new energy, new materials, energy conservation and environment protection, and new-energy automobiles.

— Constant improvement of the city function. Since 2000, Shanghai has aimed to construct 'four centers' and kept improving the city function so as to realize the target of a modernized international metropolis. In terms of becoming an international financial center, Shanghai takes the construction of a financial market system as the core, and the construction of a financial institution system as the key point. In order to foster a favorable financial environment, Shanghai actively promotes financial innovation and reform and opening up, and succeeds in making breakthroughs. By the end of 2012, the turnover of the Shanghai Stock Exchange was ranked second in Asia and fourth in the world, with the amount of funds raised ranking first in Asia and third in the world. By the end of 2011, the total amount of spot trading at the Shanghai Gold Exchange was Rmb4.44tn, retaining its leading position in the world. As an international shipping center, which takes the construction of a modern shipping service system as the core and the building of an international shipping development pilot zone as the breakthrough, conspicuous progress has been made in actively promoting policy implementation and innovation breakthrough.

Column 1-6 The global status of Shanghai's finance and shipping industries

(1) The status of finance. The 2012 'Xinhua-Dow Jones International Financial Center Development' (IFCD) showed that the comprehensive ranking of Shanghai was in sixth place, the same as in 2011. The 'growth and development' index ranked first for the third successive year. The top 10 cities were New York, London, Tokyo, Hong Kong, Singapore, Shanghai, Frankfurt, Paris, Zurich and Chicago.

(2) The status of the shipping industry. In 2011, Shanghai port became the first in the world to record a container throughput of more than 30m TEU, when it topped the world in both general cargo and container throughout.

- The accelerating pace of city infrastructure. Since 2000, the construction of Shanghai's infrastructure has been greatly accelerated, and the successful bid to host the World Expo raised higher requirements for city construction in Shanghai. From 2000 to 2012, the accumulated investment in Shanghai city infrastructure totaled Rmb1.383902tn, 4.2 times more than the investment of Rmb330.12bn between 1985 and 2000. For instance, in 2000, there were only two city subway lines, with an operational length of 62.92km, while in 2012 there were 13 city subway lines, with a total operational length of more than 468km, increasing by 7.4 times.

- Success in hosting the World Exposition. Expo 2010 was held in Shanghai between May 1 and October 31, 2010, and it was the first of the 41 World Expos to be held in a developing country. Shanghai World Expo, with its theme being 'Better City, Better Life', set a new record for the World Expo in terms of the number of participating countries, regions and international organizations (240), and the number of visitors (more than 70m). Hosting the World Expo exerted a permanent influence on the development of Shanghai, bringing a precious historic opportunity to the new-round development of Shanghai and greatly upgrading Shanghai's influence worldwide.

In the 30 years from 1978 to 2008, the rapid development of Shanghai's economy enabled the city functions to be constantly perfected and upgraded, and its international status to gradually rise and comprehensive competitiveness to continuously grow. As a result, Shanghai developed from being a domestic industrial and commercial city since the founding of the New China to a key city in the Asian-Pacific region, developed in finance, shipping and trade.

> **Column 1-7 Shanghai's ranking among global cities**
>
> (1) Shanghai ranked seventh in terms of the comprehensive strength of cities worldwide, according to the Globalization and World Cities research group and network.
>
> (2) Shanghai ranked 20th, according to the 2010 global city ranking jointly issued by *Foreign Policy* magazine in the US, AT Kearney and the Chicago Council on Global Affairs.
>
> (3) Shanghai ranked 43rd, according to the 2012 Survey Report of the Most Competitive Cities Worldwide issued by *The Economist*.
>
> (4) In a list headed by New York, Shanghai was the 21st most influential commercial center in the world, according to the 2012 Cosmopolis Index Report.

Although the 2008 global financial crisis had an impact on Shanghai's economy, the city managed to address it. In this period, Shanghai was in a post-industrial stage in which its per capita GDP exceeded Rmb10,000. Also in this stage, some bottlenecks gradually became conspicuous: the restriction of resources was more and more pressing; business costs kept rising; and the traditional growth model was unsustainable. Shanghai was in a critical period of transformation from the investment-driven model to the innovation-driven model. Since the 12th five-year plan of national economy and social development, Shanghai has implemented a strategy of 'innovation driving development, economic transition upgraded', by which Shanghai will convert the traditional economic development mode, take advantage of technological progress and innovation, attach more importance to the quality and efficiency of development, and strive to improve the comprehensiveness, harmony and sustainability of development.

With the further development of China's economy in the future and with the transfer of the world economic focus 'from west to east', it is likely that the economic power of Shanghai will be further reinforced and the city functions will be further improved. By 2020, Shanghai will have been built into an international financial center, international shipping center, international trade center and international economic center, and Shanghai will have grown up into a socialist modernized international metropolis, moving towards becoming a global city endowed with the capability of global resource allocation and administrative functions.

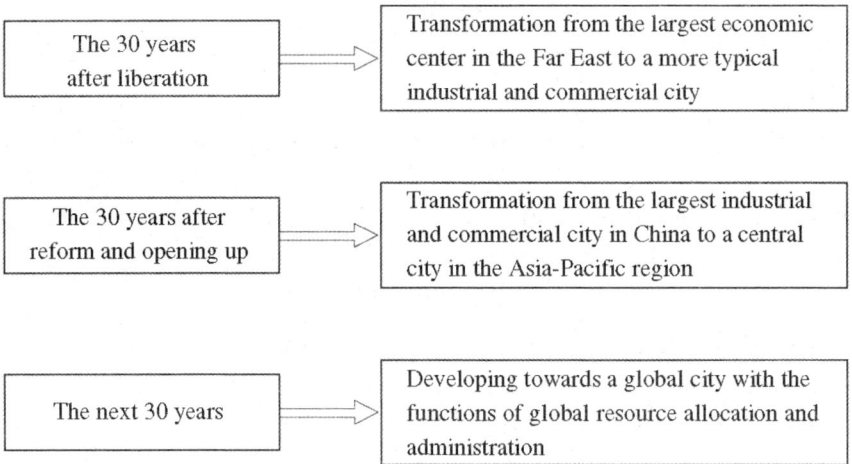

Figure 1-6 The transformation of Shanghai's city functions

Chapter 2

The Development and Transformation of Shanghai's Economy

After the founding of the New China, with the reform of its economic system and the transformation of its economic structure, the economic development of Shanghai has been constantly promoted. Shanghai experienced its first transformation at the beginning of the founding of the New China; the second happened at the end of the 1980s; and the third transformation took place after the outbreak of the 2008 international financial crisis. With these three transformations, relying on global resources, Shanghai has been able to keep upgrading itself by participating in international competition, and to change from a single-function city to a multi-function economic center based on finance, shipping and trade. This chapter illustrates the progress Shanghai has made in the construction of 'four centers', the development of a service economy and the improvement of independent innovation. It also elaborates on the main ideas regarding how to develop Shanghai in the future, and the reform measures to be taken in some key economic fields.

I. Building the 'four centers'

Through elementary construction in the 1990s and priority promotion at the beginning of the 21st century, the building of the 'four centers' has continued to make progress and breakthroughs, thereby forming the basic framework of centers of international economy, finance, trade and shipping.

1. The international center tends to be multilayered and diversified

First, the scale of the financial sector keeps growing. The financial industry in Shanghai experienced two phases of rapid development from 1995 to 1997, and from 2004 to 2007. In 2007, the added value of the financial sector amounted to Rmb120.908bn. Second, the financial market system has been established at a preliminary level. Today, financial institutions in Shanghai are increasingly diversified, and financial markets such as the monetary market, securities market, foreign exchange market, futures market and financial leasing market have all been established, which shows that the financial market system has been basically formed. Third, the influence of the financial industry in Shanghai keeps growing. With continued reform, the financial industry in Shanghai keeps developing, and its status both home and abroad keeps rising. In 2012, stock trading turnover of the Shanghai Stock Exchange ranked fourth in the world, and the market value of shares ranked seventh; the number of traded contracts on Shanghai Futures Exchange ranked second in the world, and Shanghai is one of the three global pricing centers of nonferrous metals; the spot gold

Table 2-1 The added value in Shanghai's financial industry[1]

Year	Added value in the financial industry (billion Rmb)	Added value in the tertiary industry (billion Rmb)	GDP (billion Rmb)	Proportion of added value of financial industry in added value of the tertiary industry (%)
1995	24.545	102.0.2	249.943	24.05
1996	34.784	129.211	295.755	26.92
1997	45.963	159.274	343.879	28.85
1998	51.221	185.536	380.109	27.61
1999	57.756	212.96	418.873	27.12
2000	60.295	248.686	477.117	27.55
2001	61.999	272.894	521.012	19.39
2002	58.467	303.89	574.103	19.24
2003	62.474	340.419	669.423	18.35
2004	61.245	409.726	807.283	14.95
2005	67.512	477.62	924.766	14.14
2006	82.52	550.848	1057.224	14.98
2007	120.908	682.111	1249.401	17.72
2008	141.421	787.223	1406.987	17.96
2009	180.428	893.085	1504.645	20.2
2010	195.096	983.351	1716.598	19.84
2011	227.74	1111.106	1919.569	20.50
2012	245.036	1219.915	2018.172	20.09

[1] Source: *Shanghai Statistical Yearbook*

turnover on Shanghai Gold Exchange ranked first in the world. Fourth, the clustering of financial institutions has accelerated. National and international financial institutions such as the Shanghai headquarters of the People's Bank of China and the China headquarters of Morgan Stanley have settled in Shanghai, and some quasi financial institutions and new-type financial institutions such as private equity funds, venture capital funds, financing guarantee firms, financial leasing companies and micro-credit companies have developed rapidly. By the end of 2012, there were 1,124 financial institutions in Shanghai, which was 514 more than in 2005. In the meantime, some functional business centers were also established, such as capital operation centers and data centers, which made Shanghai the 'brain' of regional financial operations. Fifth, there have been achievements in financial innovation. Innovations of some financial products have been constantly promoted, such as stocks, bonds, gold, foreign exchange and futures. Today, Shanghai is one of the areas in China where financial products are most abundant.

2. The international shipping center is motivated by two factors

Since the start of the 21st century, Shanghai has made great progress in both soft power and the hardware environment of its seaports and airports. Seaport construction has developed considerably. At present, there are 16 large-scale container berths and four branch container berths in Waigaoqiao port area, with an annual container throughput of more than 15m TEU; the first stage of the phase three project at Yangshan deepwater port has been completed, comprising 13 large-scale container berths and a container throughput of more than 7m standard containers; the phase one and phase two dredging projects of Yangtze estuary deepwater channel have been finished, creating a depth of 13 meters. General cargo throughput in the port of Shanghai rose from 85m tons in 1980 to 736m tons in 2012; international standard container throughput soared from 30,000 TEU to 32.529m TEU.

The construction of an airport hub has also made great progress. Pudong international airport expansion project was completed in 2007, when it achieved international freight hub status. Leading international express delivery firms, UPS and DHL, have settled in Pudong airport, making it the only airport in the world to accommodate two international transfer centers, resulting in the reinforcement of the air hub function. In 2007, Shanghai's annual passenger throughput broke through 50m, reaching

51.566m passenger journeys. In 2012, annual passenger throughput at Shanghai's airports stood at 78.7084m, accounting for 12.02% of China's total throughput. In the same year, cargo throughput at Shanghai airports totaled 3.3796m tons, with Pudong airport cargo transport ranking third in the world.

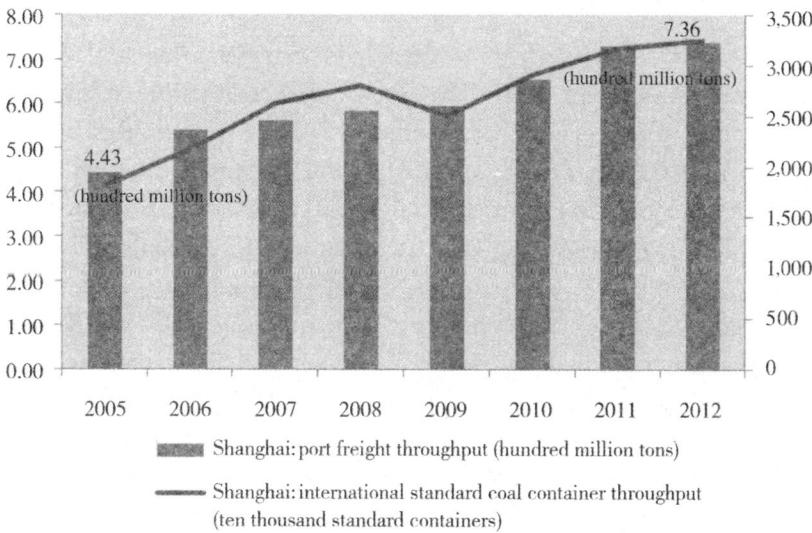

Figure 2-1 Freight volume growth at Shanghai port, 1995-2012
Source: *Shanghai Statistical Yearbook*

3. International trade center shows its first sign of prosperity

Shanghai has gradually established itself as a port trade center, accounting for an increasing share of national imports and exports. At the initial stage of reform and opening up, due to a change of the foreign trade system, Shanghai port actually experienced a fall in its share of national commodity imports and exports. At the beginning of the 21st century, as a result of the constant development of its international trade center, Shanghai's proportion kept rising, accounting for 27.4% in 2012.

A second development is Shanghai's reputation as a shopping paradise. From the perspective of total market consumption, Shanghai's total volume of retail sales of consumer goods was Rmb8.043bn in 1980, rising to Rmb741.23bn in 2012, giving an annual increase of 15.18%. The total volume of retail sales of consumer goods in Shanghai has always been one of the highest in the country. Shanghai has agglomerated thousands of internationally famous brands. More than 1,000 famous national and global brands can be found on Nanjing Road

West and its malls such as Westgate Mall, Citic Square and Plaza 66, including more than 50 top-level and premium global brands. Huaihai Road business area, another center for international brands, has vigorously tried to attract international fashion brands to set up their China headquarters. The Bund is another place where international luxury brands cluster, particularly at 18 The Bund and 3 The Bund.

The third development is Shanghai's emergence as an international purchase transaction center. In 1999, the transaction volume of the commodity trade market was Rmb66.451bn, rising to Rmb1.095915tn in 2012, giving an average annual growth rate of 9.15%. In 2006, the International Sourcing Fair annually held by Shanghai Convention and Exhibition Center was upgraded to a national-level exhibition sponsored by the Ministry of Commerce and Shanghai municipal government. It is the largest international 'reverse procurement' event in China. At the 2008 Shanghai International Sourcing Fair, major global retailers such as Wal-Mart, Tesco and B&Q set up booths to conduct 'reverse procurement', while in a similar trading forum of auto parts at Anting Automobile Exhibition Center, dozens of national and international auto parts enterprises gathered to negotiate and purchase. With the development of the exhibition industry, famous brand exhibitions have started to appear, prominent among which are the East China Fair and International Industry Fair. In addition, sourcing centers of transnational corporations are aggregating in Shanghai.

The basic framework of the 'four centers' has been formed, with the physical infrastructure reaching an international standard. As far as an international financial center is concerned, the presence of foreign banks and the cluster of various financial institutions and regulators have both acquired remarkable achievements. The port infrastructure required to build an international shipping center is comparatively sound, meeting the qualifications of an international shipping center. The commercial facilities and brand aggregation needed to create an international trade center are close to reaching an advanced world level, while in terms of exhibition facilities, more effort is needed to match international-standard exhibition halls.

II. Forming an industrial structure focused on the service economy

Since the start of reform and opening up, the industrial structure of Shanghai has experienced the three stages of adaptive adjustment, strategic adjustment and the linked development of the secondary and tertiary industries. As a result, the industrial structure focused on heavy industry has been changed, and the relative proportion of the tertiary sector has been constantly raised, which serves as an important material support for the construction of Shanghai as an international metropolis and as the center of the international economy, trade, finance and shipping.

> **Column 2-1 What is a service economy?**
>
> Service economy refers to an economic state in which the output value of the service economy is more than 60% of GDP, or to put it in another way, the service economy provides more than 60% of employment in the national economy. The service economy covers social services in which enterprises play the main role, such as logistics, finance, postal services, telecommunications, transportation, tourism, sports, commerce and trade, catering, property management, information and culture. It also covers public services mainly provided by the government and institutions, such as education, medical treatment and public health, population and family planning, and social security provision.

In 1978, Shanghai was at the initial stage of reform and opening up, and the proportion of added value of the three industries was 4.0:77.4:18.6, and the proportion of employment was 34.5:44.1:21.4, which shows that the industrial structure was imbalanced, with priority given to secondary industry while the tertiary industry was left far behind. With such an industrial structure, the conflict between economic development and public life was rather sharp, and the city function of Shanghai was just a simple production function.[2] In order to tackle the conflict between economic development and people's living needs, and in order to get Shanghai to break away from a distorted industrial development, Shanghai municipal government took a series of measures to promote the development of the tertiary industry, making adaptive adjustments to the industrial structure.

In December 1992, Shanghai had its original guideline of industrial development changed from 'secondary, tertiary, primary' to 'tertiary, secondary, primary', giving priority to the service industry and realizing the strategic adjustment of industrial structure for the three sectors. During this

---

[2] Yuan Enzhen, *Thirty Years of Shanghai: Reform and Opening Up and Economic Development* [M], Shanghai: Shanghai University of Finance and Economics Press, 2008, p.14

period, the tertiary industry developed rapidly, as shown by the fact that the proportion of the output value of the tertiary industry in 1999 outweighed that of the secondary industry. Moreover, in 2000 the number of people employed in the tertiary industry exceeded that of the secondary industry for the first time.

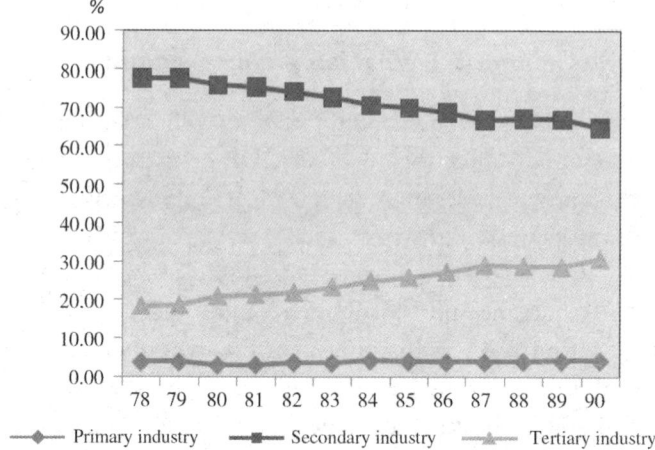

Figure 2-2 (1) The proportion of output value of the three industries in Shanghai, 1978-1990
Source: Shanghai Statistical Yearbook

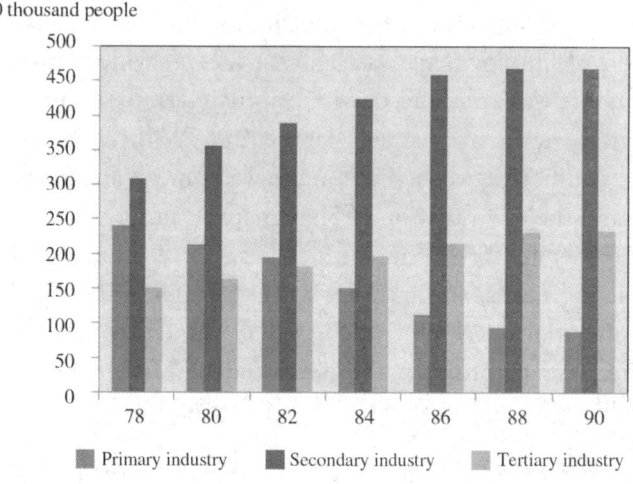

Figure 2-2 (2) The employment proportion of the three industries in Shanghai, 1978-1990
Source: Shanghai Statistical Yearbook

During the 21st century, Shanghai's tertiary industry has gradually grown into a service industry system in which the modern service industry is the orientation, with traditional service industry as the support, and the financial, insurance, trade, catering, shipping and storage, and real estate as the backbone. In 2012, the proportion of the tertiary industry in Shanghai reached 60.4%.

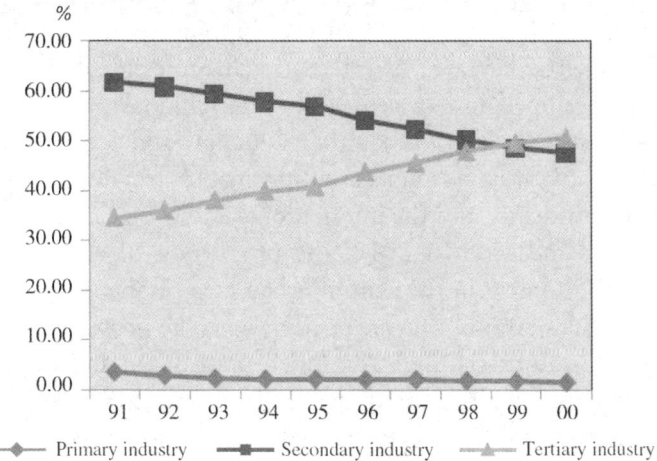

Figure 2-3(1) The proportion of output value of the three industries in Shanghai, 1991-2000

Source: Shanghai Statistical Yearbook

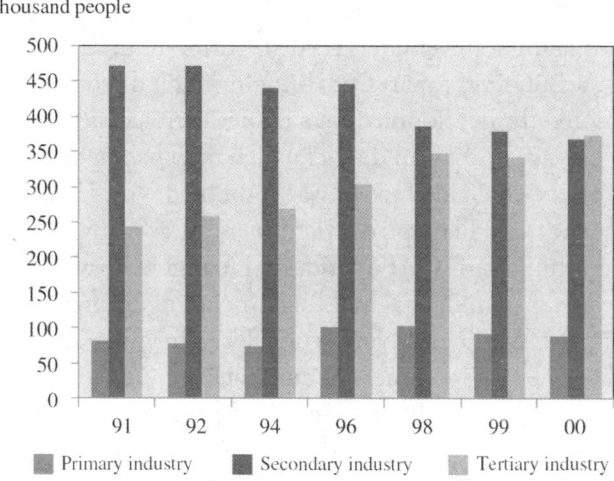

Figure 2-3(2) The employment proportion of the three industries in Shanghai, 1991-2000

Source: Shanghai Statistical Yearbook

The main measures taken to develop the service economy in Shanghai cover the following four aspects:

(1) Taking the central urban area as the pivot to drive the development of the tertiary industry

During the 21st century, Shanghai has further accelerated the development of the service industry, especially the modern service industry, making breakthroughs in finance, shipping and information. Huangpu district, relying on its unique locational advantage, has developed into the 'brain' of the shipping service industry; Jing'an district, the key area of international professional service industry, has developed into a center for international professional services such as advertising, accountancy, design and legal services. Xuhui district, with its hospitals and universities, has developed the health service industry and the international communication and education services industry. In 2012, the proportion of added value of the service industry in the central urban area of Shanghai accounted for more than 80% of that area's GDP, with the proportion in Huangpu and Jing'an exceeding 90%. The central urban area has become the engine driving the rapid development of the service industry in Shanghai, and has taken the lead in forming an industrial structure that focuses on the service industry.

(2) Striving to develop the commercial real estate economy

In 2010, there were as many as 50 commercial buildings in Shanghai whose annual revenue exceeded Rmb100m. These 'Rmb100m-revenue buildings', apart from bringing in high profits, have effectively promoted the development of a modern service industry in Shanghai. For instance, in Luwan district which only has an area of 7.54 square kilometers (in 2011, Luwan was combined with Huangpu district to create the new Huangpu district), there are as many as 15 'Rmb100m-revenue buildings'. On both sides of Huanghai Road in Luwan district, there are 23 commercial buildings, including Shanghai Central Plaza, Enterprise World and New World Plaza forming a cluster. The taxes paid by these 23 commercial buildings account for 50% of the total revenue of Luwan district. In addition, the commercial real estate economy has stimulated the rapid development of supporting service industries in the neighboring area such as catering and entertainment, which show a more conspicuous clustering effect. The 'commercial real estate economy' has become the vehicle of the development of Shanghai's modern service industry, since the more prosperous the commercial buildings, the more thriving the service industry. An improved service industry is appealing to transnational corporations and headquarter enterprises, thus driving forward the rapid development of the service industry.

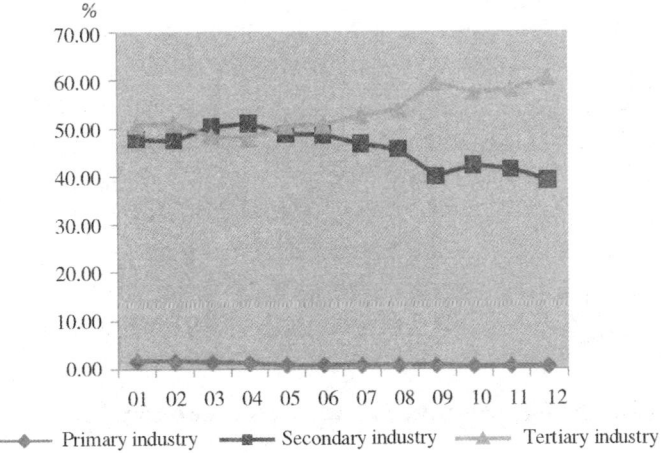

Figure 2-4 (1) The proportion of output value of the three industries in Shanghai, 2001-2012
Source: Shanghai Statistical Yearbook

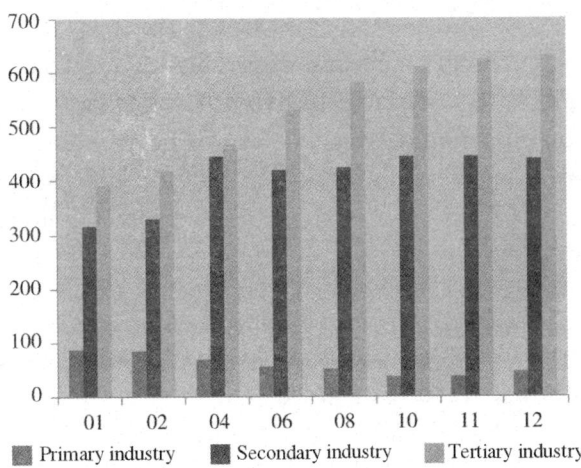

Figure 2-4 (2) The employment proportion of the three industries in Shanghai, 2001-2012
Source: Shanghai Statistical Yearbook

> **Column 2-2 What is the commercial real estate economy?**
>
> The commercial real estate economy is a new economic state that has burgeoned in recent years with China's urban economic development. It is an economic state that takes commercial buildings, buildings with different functions and regional facilities as the main carriers, and introduces enterprises by means of developing and leasing buildings in order to introduce tax sources to motivate the development of the regional economy. It is characterized by intensive pattern and high density, and mainly represented by modern services, such as finance, consultancy, advertising planning, film and television production, internet companies, law, accountancy, intermediary consultancy, high-technology, entertainment, real estate, travel services, and transportation and communication.

(3) Striving to develop the headquarters economy

By the end of 2012, Shanghai had managed to attract 265 investment companies and 403 regional headquarters of transnational corporations, the most of any city in China. At the beginning of 2007, Shanghai Promotion Center of Headquarters Economy issued the first map of the headquarters economy, designating 16 'headquarters economy' bases with access to priority support, which cover the districts of Putuo, Qingpu, Songjiang, Minhang, Zhabei, Baoshan and Jiading, along with the traditional districts of Pudong, Luwan, Changning, Jing'an and Xuhui. Such a layout maps a 'headquarters economy' strategy that is 'blooming everywhere'. The rapid development of a headquarters economy may further show the radiation effect of the city functions of Shanghai.

(4) Striving to foster the development of a cultural and creative industry and information service industry

After years of development, the radiation effect of cultural and creative industry clusters in Shanghai keeps expanding, and in some areas a comparatively complete industrial state has taken initial shape. As the economic orientation shifts gradually from manufacturing to services, the scale of the information service industry in Shanghai has continued to grow. Since 2005, the operating income of the information service industry in Shanghai has maintained a growth rate of more than 20%, and in 2012 it generated an operating income of Rmb259.395bn, with added value amounting to Rmb203.024bn which accounted for 10.1% of the city's total GDP, thus making it one of fastest growing areas of the modern service industry in Shanghai.

> **Column 2-3 What is a headquarters economy?**
>
> A headquarters economy is defined as an economic state in which a certain region, due to its sufficiently rich resources, attracts a cluster of corporate headquarters. Consequently, it brings about labor division and coordination as well as an optimal allocation of resources, by means of the development of the area where the manufacturing base is located, which is motivated by the functional radiation of 'a headquarters manufacturing base'. Developing a headquarters economy may bring many economic effects to regional development, such as tax income, multiplier effect of industries, consumption effect, employment effect and social capital effect. The settlement of a large number of headquarters of both national and international enterprises may improve the popularity and reputation of the region, urges the regional government to improve the service quality and optimize the commercial environment, improve the city infrastructure and human settlement, promotes the integration and interaction of multiple cultures, and accelerates the internationalized development of the city.

Looking to the future, Shanghai will continue to follow the targets of high-end orientation, intensification and 'servitization', promoting the integrated development of 'primary, secondary and tertiary' industries, giving great impetus to the strategic adjustment of industrial structure, in which the service economy dominates and where the industrial layout could be optimized. In addition, Shanghai also keeps improving its industrial core competitiveness, working hard to forge the 'Shanghai service'.

III. Reinforcing independent innovation capability and the construction of an innovative city

During the 11th 'five-year plan', Shanghai proposed a target of building a city innovation system focusing on independent innovation, unswervingly promoting the strategy of 'developing the city by science and education'. In 2012, the proportion of R&D expenditure in local fiscal expenditure increased to 5.9% research and development expenditure accounting for 3.37% of Shanghai's GDP, and the average education duration of the emerging labor force increasing to 14.5 years, resulting in a conspicuous improvement in innovative capabilities.

1. Constantly improving the policy environment stimulating independent innovation

At the beginning of 2006, the central government issued *Outline of the National Program for Long- and Medium-term Scientific and Technological Development (2006-2020)* along with some supportive policies. Then, on the basis of the local situation, Shanghai issued 11 policy documents including *Some Supportive Policies of Implementing the 'Outline of Shanghai's Program for Long- and Medium-term Scientific and Technological Development'* (also known as '36 items'), trying to foster a policy environment that stimulates independent innovation in terms of taxation, finance, government procurement, intellectual property protection and human resource team building. For instance, enterprises can enjoy a deduction of tax amounting to 150% of the actual expenditure of technological development in the same year, which is a policy highly acclaimed by enterprises. The 'one-stop' type of service window also applies to the policy of science and technology innovation, improving the service level of science and technology, and providing more convenient services for enterprises to be independently innovative.

2. Striving to promote close connections between production, learning and research

On the basis of the strategic decision to construct Yangpu Knowledge Innovation Zone, Shanghai put forward the core idea of 'integration of three zones and joint development', which covers the three zones of university campuses, science and technology parks, and public communities. At present, among enterprises that have carried out collaboration in production, learning and research, 87.4% have signed written contracts or collaboration agreements, and 28.3% have regular and long-term collaborative partners. The collaboration of production, learning and research in Shanghai has developed and evolved from being sporadic, irregular, temporary and primary, to being more widespread, regular, stable and advanced.

> **Column 2-4 'Three-zone linkage'**
>
> The 'three-zone linkage' refers to a development pattern according to which university campus construction is combined with science park and public community development. In such a pattern, the university campus fulfils the role of knowledge innovation and talent cultivation, providing talent and intelligence support for the regional economy and society. The technology park takes responsibility for technology incubation, technology innovation and product manufacture. As the important venue of combining industry, university and research, and as the base for university teachers and students to be innovative and start businesses, the technology park has become the growth point of regional economic development. The public community takes on the function of providing public services for the university campus and the science park, creating an ecological and social environment favorable to living, communication and leisure. The relationship between the three is that the university campus is the core, the science (industry) park is the base and the urban public service is the support. The relationship is characterized by the aggregation, sharing, integration and transfer of resources, and is aimed at promoting educational development and technological innovation, so as to foster the harmonious development between universities and the urban economy and society.

3. Constantly intensifying input to the R&D of independent innovation

In 2012, R&D investment in Shanghai amounted to Rmb67.946bn, about 13.68% more than that of the previous year, and its proportion in Shanghai's GDP increased from 2.33% in 2005 to 3.37%, reaching or approaching the R&D investment level of major developed countries. R&D investment by enterprises also increased, reaching Rmb42.634bn in 2012, becoming a major impetus to the growth of R&D investment in Shanghai. In 2012, there were 1,826 companies carrying out R&D activities, accounting for 84.85% of the total number of units engaged in scientific and technological activities. The number of people engaged in R&D was 208,800, accounting for 53.69% of the total number of science and technology personnel in the whole city. In addition, the quality of those engaged in independent innovation is constantly improving.

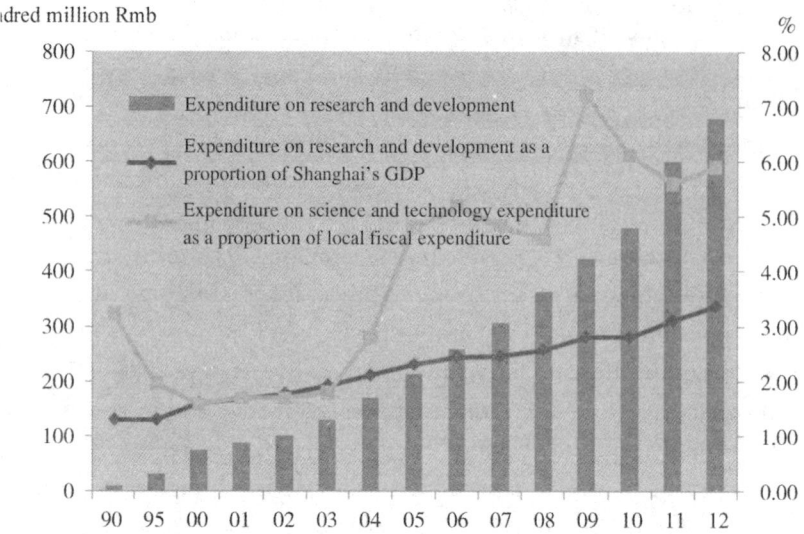

Figure 2-5 Shanghai investment in R&D, 1990 to 2012
The data source: calculated according to Shanghai Statistical Yearbook

IV. Reforming and developing the economic system with vitality

Since the start of reform and opening up, Shanghai has actively promoted economic system reform that focuses on enlivening SOEs, and has explored establishing an economic operating system that can meet the needs of a socialist market economy with Chinese characteristics, and conform to international practice, so that a system guarantee could be established for the construction of an international metropolis. Shanghai reform can be divided into three phases: the 1980s witnessed the reform of enterprises designed to stimulate these enterprises; the 1990s saw an opening up to absorb foreign investment; since 2000, a variety of systems have been established that are in line with international standards.

1. Transformation of ownership structure

After the third plenary session of the 11th Central Committee of the CPC, the non-public sectors of Shanghai's economy began to resume and develop, and over a period of 30 years, the non-public sectors of the economy have grown more vigorously, serving as a major force stimulating the economic development of Shanghai.

First, the state-owned economy still plays the leading role. Shanghai used to be the city with the greatest clustering of SOEs and the highest proportion of the state-owned economy. Through the reform of SOEs and the strategic adjustment of the national economy, state-owned capital has been inclined to invest in strategic industries and groups with competitive edge. Public ownership is gradually realized in a variety of forms, and SOEs and state-controlled enterprises are growing increasingly competitive.

Table 2-2 The importance of Shanghai's public-owned economy relative to its non-public economy

unit:%

Aggregate indicators	1978	2012	2012: 1978 (plus or minus)
Gross value of production (public-owned: non-public)	99:1	49.3:50.7	Public-owned: -49.7 Non-public: +49.7
State-owned economy	86.2	44.6	-41.6
Fixed-asset investment (public-owned: non-public)	96.9:3.1	37.45:62.55	Public-owned: -59.45 Non-public: +59.45
State-owned economy	85.4	35.31	-50.09
Retail sales of consumer goods (public-owned: non-public)	99.6:0.4	5.98:94.02	Public-owned: -93.62 Non-public: +93.62
State-owned economy	73.0	4.27	-68.73
Number of employees (public-owned: non-public)	100:0	116.32:83.68	Public-owned: -83.68 Non-public: +83.68
State-owned economy	79.5	14.99	-64.51

Sources: 1978 data, see: Zuo Xuejin, *Shanghai Economic Reform and City Development: Practice and Experience* [M], Shanghai: Shanghai Academy of Social Sciences Press, 2008, p.29. 2012 data, see: *Shanghai Statistical Yearbook 2013*. 'Public-owned economy' refers to 'state-owned economy plus collective economy', and 'non-public economy' refers to the remainder

Second, foreign capital has become the most vibrant element in the multiple structure of ownership that exists in Shanghai. At the end of the 1970s, in order address the lack of both capital and technology, Deng Xiaoping put forward a major initiative to attract foreign capital. The very first joint venture in Shanghai was a Shanghai-Hong Kong joint venture, Shanghai United Wool Textile, which was founded on August 4, 1981 in Lujiazui, Pudong. Since then, a large number of Hong Kong business people have invested in Shanghai; investment from and via the Hong Kong region has always ranked first in terms of the number of projects and the amount of investment. By the end of 2012, foreign direct investment contracts in Shanghai had totaled 67,869, with a contract value of US$217.565bn and utilized foreign investment of US$134.213bn.

Table 2-3 The proportion of leading indicators of Shanghai's SOEs across the whole city

unit: %

	Enterprises	Practitioners	Total assets at year end	Total profit	Total tax
2000	3.9	31.0	59.1	54.8	64.1
2001	3.9	29.4	60.6	52.5	63.5
2002	4.0	26.2	52.6	57.1	64.1
2003	2.3	21.3	46.7	56.1	62.7
2004	12.3	28.0	51.3	59.0	70.8
2005	2.4	16.6	44.0	49.4	61.0
2006	9.4	20.8	49.0	51.9	65.4
2007	7.7	17.9	48.6	50.0	66.6
2008	6.3	16.5	48.1	34.7	61.2
2009	6.2	16.6	48.8	48.1	68.8
2010	6.1	15.9	46.3	49.2	72.2
2011	8.1	17.7	46.0	50.7	73.2
2012	7.9	17.5	45.4	52.3	72.3

Source: *Shanghai Statistical Yearbook*

Third, the shareholding economy has developed rapidly. On November 4, 1984, Shanghai Feiyue Stereo Company was spun off from Shanghai Feiyue Electroacoustic Factory and transformed into a limited liability company. With approval from the Shanghai branch of People's Bank of China, it took the lead in a pilot stockholding project and became the first company in Shanghai to issue stocks, 10,000 in total with a face value of Rmb50. Afterwards, this pilot project was applied to some medium-sized enterprises. Unlike traditional industries with a single ownership structure, joint-stock enterprises have developed rapidly due to their multiple property rights and flexible mixed nature. In 1995, joint stock enterprises accounted for only 5.3% of all domestic enterprises in Shanghai, but the proportion increased to 36.9% in 2001, and in the first half of 2007, they accounted for 88%. By the end of 2012, altogether 2,494 companies listed in mainland China (A shares and B shares), of which 248 were Shanghai companies, accounting for 9.94% of the total.

Fourth, the private sector of the economy started to show its vitality. Under pressure from powerful state-owned companies and foreign investors, the private economy has managed to survive and prosper, accounting for an increasing share of both industrial complementation and employment. In 2012, revenue from the private economy in Shanghai was Rmb193.32bn, accounting for 26.2% of the city's total revenue; its GDP was Rmb537.937bn, accounting for 27% of the total; investment was Rmb155.238bn, accounting for 29.5% of the total amount of fixed asset investment in the whole society. The private economy also became more important in terms of employment.

Table 2-4 Numbers employed by Shanghai's private enterprises

Unit: ten thousand persons

	Urban employees		Rural employees	
	Private enterprises	Total	Private enterprises	Total
1992	1.2	536.24	5.3	270.67
1995	28.2	537.6	14.6	230.4
2000	58.23	417.51	92.69	255.6
2005	256.73	612.37	209.08	243.49
2006	259.76	615.45	213.15	—
2007	266.4	657.82	209.93	218.76
2008	282.63	682.17	230.27	211.1
2009	311.1	723.52	237.15	205.72
2010	314.1	736	258.4	188.7
2011	337.48	—	278.66	—

Source: *China Statistical Yearbook*.

2. Fiscal and taxation system reform

Prior to reform and opening up, China's fiscal system was highly centralized, and the fiscal revenue and expenditure of both the central and local government were under 'unified control'. Under this system, Shanghai handed over a large amount of revenue to the central government, making great contributions to the national fiscal revenue. Between 1959 and 1978, the amount of revenue Shanghai handed over to the country was 25 times the net value of the city's fixed assets. Take 1978 as an example. In that year, Shanghai's local fiscal revenue was Rmb195.24bn, while the amount handed over to the central government was Rmb166.67bn. In spite of its great contributions to the whole country, Shanghai was rather backward in terms of city construction and the improvement of its residents' living conditions.

For instance, Shanghai ranked last nationally in terms of road area per capita and living area per capita, and pollution control over the 'three wastes' (waste water, air pollution and waste residue) also ranked last.

After the third plenary session of the 11th Central Committee of the CPC, China began to promote overall reform and opening up, and the fiscal and taxation system also survived the trend of 'grand unification'. In the 1980s, Shanghai played the role of 'full back' in the whole pattern of reform and opening up, bearing responsibility for providing financial and personnel support for the pilot sections and regions.

In November 1993, the third session of the 14th Central Committee of the CPC passed *On Some Issues Concerning Establishing the Socialist Market Economy System*, clearly putting forward the 'tax distribution system' principle that was based on a reasonable division of central and local functions and powers, to take the place of the original fiscal system of fixed contract. During this period, Shanghai came to establish and improve its own tax distribution system. As early as the end of the 1980s, Shanghai began to set about establishing a two-level fiscal system comprising municipal level and district level. After the 1990s, Shanghai began to explore the feasibility of city administration and construction with 'two-level governments, two-level administration', trying in several stages to devolve office authority powers, financial control powers and administration powers to districts and counties, and in 1994 began transfer payment between the municipal government and the district and county governments. Tax distribution reform in Shanghai stimulated local government initiatives, laying solid foundations for the city's economic development and social progress. Shanghai's fiscal revenue and expenditure also experienced significant growth, particularly after 2002.

In the 17th National Party Congress of the CPC, the planned reform of the taxation system was clearly put forward, which attached importance to harmonious development and concern for people's livelihoods, and the implementation of a tax system favorable to scientific development. On November 16, 2011, with the ratification of the State Council, the Ministry of Finance and State Administration of Taxation jointly issued the *Pilot Plan of Levying VAT Instead of Business Tax*, announcing that from January 1, 2012, pilot projects would levy value added tax (VAT) instead of business tax in Shanghai in the transportation and some modern service industries. Since then, Shanghai has managed to transform its taxation system by means of the 'VAT instead of business tax' policy. Some 126,000 enterprises have

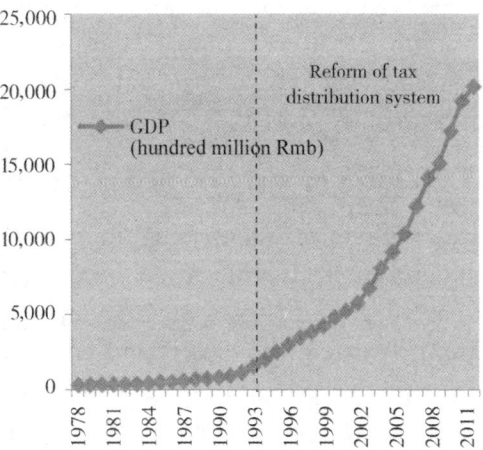

Figure 2-6(1) Shanghai's GDP 1978-2012

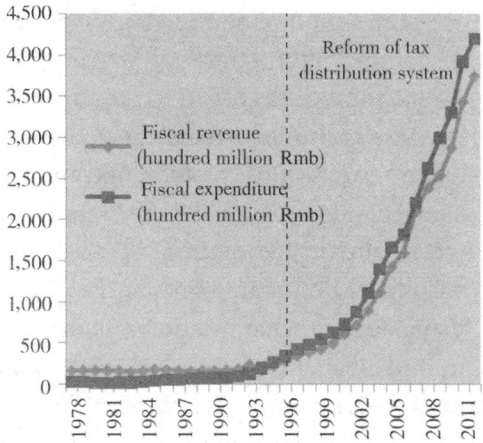

Figure 2-6(2) Shanghai's financial revenue and expenditure 1978-2012

been involved in the pilot projects (including 11,000 in transportation, 115,000 in modern service industry, along with 40,000 general taxpayers and 86,000 small-scale taxpayers), and these enterprises and the former ordinary VAT payers have been relieved of a tax burden totaling Rmb4.45bn. In the meantime, Shanghai stimulated the creation of an industrial structure focusing on the service industry, by means of the 'VAT instead of business tax' policy. In the first half of 2012, when there was negative growth in the real estate industry, the value added of Shanghai's tertiary industry increased by 10.3% year-on-year, accounting for 60.4% of the gross domestic product of the whole city, which was 2.6% up on the same period of the previous year. There has been an ever-growing tendency among international multinational enterprises to invest in Shanghai, especially in modern service industries. In 2012, 50 multinational enterprises established their regional headquarters in Shanghai, and over the same period, there were 25 newly established investment companies and 14 R&D centers.

3. Reform of state-owned assets and enterprises

In the 30 years of reform and opening up in Shanghai, the reform of state-owned assets and enterprises has always been the core, and in each phase of reform and opening up, the government would make specific arrangements for the reform of state-owned assets and enterprises. The reform of state-owned assets and enterprises in Shanghai may be divided into four phases: devolution of administrative powers, establishment of the administrative system of state-owned assets and enterprises, establishment of the modern enterprise system, and establishment of the modern property rights system.

Phase one: devolution of administrative powers (1978 to 1987). Under the influence of the reform idea of the separation of the government's executive powers, some SOEs began to acquire self-management powers, and the state-owned assets also came to be transferred from the original centralized and central administration to the local and ministry administration, which gradually changed the situation where state-owned assets and enterprises were highly centralized. 'Devolution' became the major approach of SOE reform in this phase, deeply influencing the direction and progress of SOE reform in Shanghai. Shanghai promoted pilot reform of the enterprise joint stock system and liberalized operation, and in addition, the pilot reform of administrative companies was carried out in electromechanical and medicine bureaus, with the administrative function that used to be fulfilled by the enterprise turned over to competent government departments, while production and management authority was further delegated to the enterprise. Some social affairs were delegated to the district or county government under the territorial principle, so as to try to separate government functions from enterprise management, and separate the government as public administrator from government as state-owned assets administrator. However, the enterprise lacks independence because it is still attached to the government, and the incentive function of the reform was rather limited. Following the success of the rural family contract responsibility system, some competent departments of Shanghai municipal government suggested that the contracting system should be introduced in the reform of industrial and commercial enterprises, with a contract signed between the government and enterprise management, and the rights and obligations of the enterprise well defined. However, the contracting system resulted in an even more obscure definition of the property rights of enterprises and, therefore, the conflict of interest between the government and enterprises became more severe, with acts of infringement happening all the time.

Phase two: establishing the state-owned assets and SOE administration system (1988 to 1997). This period witnessed the rapid development of all types of non-public economy, which exerted unprecedented competitive pressure on SOEs and urged the government to consider how to further improve the operating performance of SOEs. In 1993, Shanghai took the lead in establishing the State-owned Assets Supervision and Administration Commission of Shanghai municipal government, exploring the effective separation of the government's ownership function from its other functions so as to preserve and increase the value of state-owned assets. After the 14th National Congress of the CPC, Shanghai formed its state-owned assets management framework of 'two-level management', 'two systems' and 'three layers', on the basis of the principle of 'being owned by the country, managed by different levels of government and autonomously operated by enterprises'. In this way, an asset's responsibility pattern took initial shape, in which the government was responsible for assets management, the group for assets operation and the enterprise for production and operation.

Phase three: establishing the modern enterprise system (1998 to 2002). Over the years, the State-owned Assets Supervision and Administration Commission of Shanghai municipal government has further realized that, to enhance enterprise vitality and improve enterprise performance, it is necessary for enterprises to be granted full autonomy of operation and management, and at the same time, the supervision and administration of enterprise production and operation should be reinforced. Therefore, the following two tasks are conducted. First, reform is carried out to build a modern enterprise system in SOEs, with different enterprises exploring different ways. Second, the state-owned assets administration system is further improved, and planning and coordination by the State-owned Assets Supervision and Administration are fully strengthened to reinforce the supervisory function of the government. In this phase, the State-owned Assets Supervision and Administration Commission of Shanghai municipal government promoted the separation of government from assets and the separation of government functions from enterprise management, preliminarily establishing the investor system of state-owned assets, standardizing the reorganization and restructuring of enterprises, and thus forming the system, with Shanghai characteristics, of equity transaction administration, supervision and operation, promoting the circulation and reorganization of state-owned assets. Through the establishment of a modern enterprise system in SOEs, the corporate administration structure began to form and improve, and the pattern of diversified equities started to take initial shape.

> **Column 2-5 'Two-level administration', 'two systems' and 'three layers'**
>
> 'Two-level administration' refers to two administrators of the State-owned Assets Supervision and Administration Commission of Shanghai municipal government and Shanghai State-owned Assets Operation Co. The former is the general representative of Shanghai state-owned assets ownership, and it fulfills the administrative function as the owner of state-owned assets in Shanghai city. Shanghai State-owned Assets Administration Office is the standing body of the State Council's State-owned Assets Supervision and Administration Commission, and it is the functional department of Shanghai municipal government that is specifically in charge of the administration of state-owned assets. The latter is the state-holding company and large-scale enterprise group ratified and authorized by the State-owned Assets Supervision and Administration Commission of Shanghai municipal government, playing the proprietorship role as investor, and it is a registered special business entity engaged in assets operation.
>
> 'Two systems' refers to the operating and supervising systems of state-owned assets. The operating system is mainly represented in the activities of State-owned Assets Operation Co, while the supervising system involves the State-owned Assets Supervision and Administration Commission of Shanghai municipal government requiring the competent department to dispatch a board of supervisors to State-owned Assets Operation Co, so as to reinforce supervision to the operation of the company.
>
> As to the 'three layers', the first layer is the Municipal State-owned Assets Office, which is mainly in charge of the macroscopic operation of state-owned assets administration as a whole, that is, in charge of policy making, standard setting and direction leading. The second layer is Shanghai State-owned Assets Operation Company and large enterprise groups, while the third layer is comprised of manufacturing enterprises, engaged in product management and controlled by Shanghai State-owned Assets Operation Co.

Phase four: establishment of a modern property rights system (2003 to 2013). In order to reach the target of maintaining or increasing state-owned assets, the government came to realize it was vital that they provide guidance and cooperative support for SOEs. This philosophical change deeply influenced the reform path of the state-owned assets and enterprises in Shanghai in this period. The first move was to actively encourage the diversification of investors in SOEs, so as to acquire a variety of financing channels. In 2003, the State-owned Assets Supervision and Administration Commission of Shanghai municipal government was established, which gave priority to the stock rights diversification of state-owned groups. Since the 11th 'five-year plan', Shanghai has continued to promote the diversification of property rights subjects of SOEs, giving impetus to the securitization process of SOEs. The second was to actively promote asset circulation and asset reorganization across regions, across departments and across systems, which may cover use of the capital market to reinforce capital operations, the improvement of a property rights exchange market system and the full play of the capital operation function among state-owned companies. The third was to strategically reorganize SOEs. On April 24, 2003, Shanghai Bailian Group listed its stocks, which reflected the idea of 'scale integration' in the strategic reorganization of SOE reform. In April 2005, reform of the shareholder structure was officially initiated, and Shanghai implemented reform of the shareholder structure together with the strategic adjustment of state-owned assets and enterprises, industrial optimization and upgrade, and the expansion and growth of listed companies. Shanghai Jahwa implemented targeted share repurchases on the basis of share reform, and elevated the value of the company, winning considerable market recognition; Shenergy Company made a public offering, becoming the first company to take the second step in the three-step process of 'separating the old and the new'; Shanghai International Port (Group) by means of capital integration of the group and its subordinate holding listed companies, accelerated the pace of listing as a whole and increased the vitality of the market.

Today, state-owned assets and enterprises in Shanghai are in a new phase of 'deepening reform and improving the competitiveness of SOEs'. In December 2013, Shanghai issued *On Further Deepening Shanghai State-owned Assets to Promote Enterprise Development*, taking a further step to establish the reform target in terms of state-owned assets management, state-owned assets layout and SOEs. The specific reform targets include gradually increasing the proportion of tax revenues from the profits achieved by state-owned assets to no lower than 30% in 2020; clearly defining the function orientation of SOEs and implementing classification management by dividing Shanghai's SOEs into competitive enterprises, functional enterprises and public service enterprises, and gradually realizing the differentiated administration. The other target is that more than 80% of state capital should be concentrated in key fields and competitive industries such as strategic emerging industries, advanced manufacturing industry, modern service industry, and the fields of infrastructure and guaranteeing people's livelihoods. As a result, a number of enterprise groups, internationally competitive and influential, will be formed, including two or three capital management companies, between five and eight transnational groups, and eight-to-10 enterprise groups leading the country in terms of overall strength.

V. Constantly improving the new pattern of an open economy

1. Building china (shanghai) pilot free trade zone

China (Shanghai) Pilot Free Trade Zone is a regional free trade zone established in Shanghai by the Chinese government. It was the first free trade zone in mainland China. This pilot zone was officially authorized by the State Council on August 22, 2013, and officially started operations on 29 September. The total area of the pilot zone is 28.78 square kilometers, equivalent to 1/226 of the total area of Shanghai city, covering the following four special administration customs areas of Shanghai Waigaoqiao Bonded Area, Waigaoqiao Bonded Area logistics park, Yangshan Bonded Port Area and the Comprehensive Bonded Area of Shanghai Pudong International Airport.

The main tasks of China (Shanghai) Pilot FTZ include: accelerating the transformation of government functions; actively promoting the further opening up of the service industry and the reform of the foreign investment administration system; striving to develop a headquarters economy and new trading methods; accelerating the convertibility of capital projects and the overall opening up of the financial service industry; exploring to establish a pattern of goods supervision based on different categories; trying to establish a policy supporting system that promotes investment and innovation; and fostering the business environment of internationalization and legalization. Its target is to become a pilot free trade zone that can meet international standards, and provide convenient investment trade, free currency exchange, efficient and convenient supervision, and a well-regulated legal environment.

> **Column 2-6 Essential differences between an FTZ and FTA**
>
> An FTZ (free trade zone) is a regional economic special zone established within the territory of one country (region) according to the law and regulation of this country (region). This is a foreign trade activity within one country (or region), which means that one country (or region) marks off a specific area of land within its territory as a marketplace for foreign trade, not intervening too much in its trade activities, and offering preferential duty policies to foreign goods. China (Shanghai) Pilot Free Trade Zone is one such FTZ.
>
> An FTA (free trade area) is a traditional free trade area, the result of a regional economic trade organization established according to an agreement between many countries, including the protocol country (region). In an FTA, countries and regions (economic entities) provide a variety of preferential policies in order to promote mutual trade, while the trade rules are made jointly by partner countries on the basis of the international agreement.

China (Shanghai) Pilot FTZ is the paramount measure taken to deepen reform and opening up, and further policies include reform and breakthrough in the transformation of government functions, the exploration of innovative modes of administration, and the promotion of trade and investment. For instance, the opening of investment has expanded, and the 'negative list' of investment areas has been established. The negative list of the 2013 version of China (Shanghai) Pilot FTZ covers all 18 economic industries in the national economy, involving 89 large categories, 419 medium-sized categories and 1,069 small categories, with special administration measures applying to 190 items. In areas outside the negative list, the check and approval process of foreign investment projects has been amended to a filing system (domestic investment projects are still checked and approved according to State Council rules). In the meantime, through the systematic assessment of current industries and policies, taking into account the characteristics of China's economic and industrial development, and on the basis of the change of foreign investment policies, the requirement to expand into new areas and the development needs of the pilot free zone, Shanghai has also made constant adjustments to the negative list. For instance, the special administration measures in the 2014 version of the negative list have been reduced to 139 items.

> **Column 2-7 The negative list management mode**
>
> The 'negative list management mode' is defined as a list of those economic sectors that have no access to opening up according to government regulations. All other industries, sectors and economic activities are allowed, except those fields on the list. All administrative measures specifically designed for foreign investment, which do not conform to national treatment and most-favored-nation treatment, and all administrative measures in terms of performance requirements and senior management requirements, are both written into the negative list.

Since China (Shanghai) Pilot FTZ started operations on September 29, 2013, it has made a series of system innovations, demonstrating its role in promoting opening in Shanghai and even the whole country.

(1) Attracting enterprises. The pilot FTZ has taken the lead in implementing the negative list, abolishing the administrative checks and approvals, and speeding up the system of paying registered capital, which has helped to boost the efficiency of commercial registration and attracted new enterprises. Within the first month of the establishment of the pilot FTZ, there were 208 newly registered enterprises, with a registered capital of more than Rmb3.5bn, more than four times the number of 44 enterprises that were registered in the same area in 2012. By the end of June 2014, a total of 10,445 enterprises had newly settled in Shanghai Pilot FTZ, of which 1,245 were foreign-invested enterprises.

(2) Generating the ripple effect. Shanghai established the pilot FTZ in order to establish a link between the zone and the area outside, mobilizing the new creation of an open economy for the whole city. Its ripple effect covers the four aspects of 'increase, transfer, decline and upgrade'. 'Increase' means that what cannot be done outside the zone may be done inside the zone, and therefore the development opportunities of enterprises outside the zone are increased. For instance, Shanghai International Energy Exchange was able to attract international investors to get directly involved in the trading of oil futures. 'Transfer' means that the enterprises inside the zone may move outside to conduct business, and such a transfer may relieve the problem of limited land availability inside the zone, as well as sustain the development of commercial real estate in business centers outside the zone. The third aspect is 'decline', which means lowering the cost for enterprises outside the zone in establishing offshore companies and overseas investment in Hong Kong

and Singapore. Enterprises outside the zone may directly carry out offshore operations and conduct international investment and financing based on the pilot FTZ, which may greatly reduce its cost of operations overseas. 'Upgrade' means that financial policies in the pilot FTZ may provide global fund settlement and transfer facilities for transnational enterprises, which may help these enterprises upgrade their regional headquarters to Asia-Pacific or even global headquarters.

(3) System innovation may be popularized and replicated. The core of Shanghai Pilot FTZ is system innovation rather than blindly focusing on preferential policies. The pilot zone focuses on innovation of the investment management system, operating the negative list administration; focusing on innovation of the trade supervision system, strengthening the supervision of management between the FTZ and other places within the territory; focusing on the innovation of the financial system, taking the lead in the trial of interest rate marketization and the foreign exchange management system; focusing on innovation of the integrated supervision system, deepening the reform of the public administration system. China (Shanghai) Pilot FTZ, as the origin of system innovation in China's open economy, has drawn wide international attention. A large number of foreign-owned transnational enterprises have been persuaded to start operations in China because of the pilot FTZ, which improves Shanghai's international image and competitiveness.

2. The 'introduction' of foreign capital

(1) The constantly stable scale of foreign capital employment

Since the 1980s, Shanghai has greatly promoted the introduction of foreign capital, using it to drive the city's development. After years of efforts, Shanghai has entered a comparatively 'stable' period in the employment of foreign capital, in terms of scale and structure. As long as the outside environment does not change significantly, there won't be any obvious change to the scale of capital introduction and the destination of foreign investment. In 2012, contractual foreign investment in Shanghai amounted to US$22.338bn, an increase of 11.1% over the previous year, reaching a new record. Utilized foreign capital was US$15.185bn, an increase of 20.5%, accounting for nearly one seventh of the national total.

(2) Optimization of the structure of foreign capital employment

The first aspect is 'service orientation'. In 2012, Shanghai's service industry employed foreign capital worth US$12.679bn, an increase of 21.6% on a year-on-year basis, and the proportion of foreign capital introduced by the service industry was up 83.5%. Of the service industries, the business service industry, commerce service industry and real estate industry have attracted similar amounts of foreign capital. The business service industry focuses on the headquarters economy; the commerce service industry features large-scale chain stores; the real estate industry focuses on medium- and long-term capital invested in the operation of high-end real estate. All these play positive roles in the improvement of urban economic competitiveness. The second aspect is high-end orientation. The foreign investment introduced by Shanghai manufacturing industries is gradually extending to the two ends of the 'smile curve'. The number of research and marketing enterprises in Shanghai' is continually expanding, and the new types of business also keep growing, such as operation centers, logistics centers, marketing centers, order centers and maintenance centers. Almost all the top 500 transnational enterprises and all the top 500 private enterprises in China have established headquarters or branch businesses in Shanghai.

3. Shanghai enterprises 'go global'

According to the transnational investment development cycle theory, foreign investment enters the fast growth period when per capita GDP exceeds US$5,000. Shanghai also actively promotes the 'going global' of enterprises, focusing on developing resource projects such as international raw materials and energy, encouraging the merger and acquisition of international manufacturing projects that have R&D centers and good brand names, and encouraging projects to explore overseas marketing and services. Priority is given to projects that can stimulate the exports of local products, equipment, projects and labor services.

Today, Shanghai is accelerating the pace of 'going global'. The first way it is doing this is by internationalizing foreign investment growth. In 2012, Shanghai's total amount of the foreign investment was US$3.24bn, increasing 22%, and nearly six times level of investment in 2008. Foreign investment has entered a period of fast growth, which conforms to the law of development of most developed countries. The second is the internationalization of investors. The investment mode is gradually transforming from one dominated by SOEs and which targets the acquisition of resources, to investment mainly by private enterprises and targeting the exploration of markets. Foreign investment made by private transnational enterprises accounted for more than 70% of total foreign investment. Private enterprises, centered on the market and oriented towards value maximization, are the main form of current foreign direct investment. The third way is the internationalization of investment destination. Investment is gradually transforming from vertical investment in developing areas such as Africa and Southeast Asia to horizontal investment, where developed countries are the destination. The capital bears the obvious feature of mutual flow, and such horizontal investment is aimed at acquiring markets, marketing channels and professionals from these developed countries. The fourth is the internationalization of investment mode. Investment has changed from greenfield investment to investment that is in the internationally prevailing forms of merger and capital growth. In 2012, the proportion of merger and capital growth in Shanghai's foreign investment was nearly 70%. The fifth way is the internationalization of financing mode. Due to the low cost of financing in the international finance market, international financing and local financing are frequently employed by transnational enterprises. By 2013, there were more than 100 foreign-listed enterprises, which has encouraged the establishment of overseas investment and facilitated business development overseas with international capital.

4. The 'one circle, three belts' opening up to the domestic market

With the deepening of the strategy of overall opening up of China, the concept of Shanghai as the meeting point of the west Pacific Ocean and the economic hinterland of China is playing a more conspicuous role in the opening up to the domestic market. The total investment from domestic enterprises exceeds that from foreign enterprises, which not only shows the 'great effectiveness' of Shanghai's opening up to the domestic market, with the capabilities of aggregation, radiation and service constantly improved, but also reflects the fact that more and more enterprises outside Shanghai 'go out to sea by borrowing boats' and 'ascend a height by borrowing a ladder'. Shanghai is perfecting its node role as a global city.

In terms of space, Shanghai has formed a multi-dimensional pattern of 'one circle, three belts' as far as the opening up to the domestic market is concerned. 'One circle' refers to the Yangtze River Delta, which is the core area of Shanghai's opening up to the domestic market. In 2013, the four provinces and cities in the delta region gave priority to transportation, and promoted cooperative projects in information, technology, credit, foreign affairs services, social insurance, human resources, finance, industrial transfer, environment protection, industry and commerce. The trans-provincial

Shanghai-Kunshan subway express line greatly promotes the process of urban integration. 'Three belts' refer to the economic support belt of the golden waterway of the Yangtze river that starts in Shanghai, the economic belt of the New Silk Road and the coastal economic belt that centers on Shanghai. These 'three belts' are the future growth pole of Shanghai in the opening up to the domestic market.

Chapter 3

The Innovation of Shanghai's Social Administration

Over the years, Shanghai has made conspicuous progress in social administration and social construction, and a favorable work environment and policy system framework have been preliminarily formed. Great progress has been made in the construction of a social public service system, and living conditions have been constantly improved. The world has become aware of Shanghai's growing participation in civil society. Two examples are the 2003 SARS outbreak and the 2010 World Expo, with the former being successfully conquered and the latter successfully hosted. Shanghai went through these two big events without incurring any social problems, showing the effectiveness of the city's social administration. This chapter looks at issues in the field of social administration, with priority given to Shanghai's social administration mode, community construction, social security, social undertaking and integrated population administration.

I. Innovating the social administration pattern

In November 2013, the third plenary session of the 18th Central Committee of the CPC passed *Decision of the Central Committee of the CPC on Some Key Issues of Comprehensively Deepening Reform*, in which the concept of 'social administration' was put forward clearly for the first time. It was also pointed out in the *Decision* that social administration must be implemented on the basis of maintaining the fundamental interests of the overwhelming majority of people and enhancing harmonious factors to the utmost extent, so that the vitality of social development is reinforced and social administration improved, so as to carry forward the construction of a peaceful China, the maintenance of national security, and the guarantee of a peaceful and contented life for people and the orderly and stable state of society.[1]

---

[1] *Decision of the Central Committee of the CPC on Some Key Issues of Comprehensively Deepening Reform*, passed by the third plenary session of the 18th Central Committee of the CPC, November 12, 2013

> **Column 3-1 What is the work unit system?**
>
> A work unit is a special organization designed to accommodate the planned economy system, and political, economic and social functions, characterized by administration, closure and togetherness. The country realizes the management of employees by means of the organization form of work units, and the management of the idlers in society, recipients of civil relief and social special care, thus realizing the supervision and integration of all social members in the city, and reaching the target of stabilizing society and consolidating political power.

Before reform and opening up, Shanghai took the urban grassroots administration system that gave priority to the 'work unit system', with the 'neighborhood system' playing a supplementary role. Work units bore the major functions of social administration and service, and they usually combined political, economic and social functions, covering all social aspects of those belonging to 'work units'. The individuals were highly dependent on their work units, and the social identification of individuals was also realized on the basis of the standards of work units. Neighborhood organizations played a very small part, for the country mainly carried out social organization, social mobilization and social administration through work units, and neighborhood organizations were somewhat marginalized and just carried out some supportive work, such as taking care of those who were unemployed, in receipt of government relief and entitled to preferential policies. Voluntary associations were rather underdeveloped. Since the work units undertook most social administration and service functions, voluntary associations did not have a favorable environment. In the 35 years of reform and opening up, Shanghai's municipal government and district governments were able to draw on the wisdom of civilians and make many fruitful explorations in the innovation of social construction and social administration. Shanghai has realized the leapfrog development in social development and social administration, moving towards an intellectual society and information age. After years of exploration, Shanghai has formed a comparatively sound social administration system, the major features of which are described below.

1. The reinforcement and innovation of social administration oriented towards people's livelihoods

Shanghai attaches much importance to work related to people's livelihoods, such as employment and social insurance. With the principle of trying the best according to its capabilities, and for the purpose of promoting social justice and improving public welfare, Shanghai has made a series of explorations in social administration. Positive employment policies have been implemented, and since 2000 more than 500,000 new employment positions have been created each year. The social insurance system has been constantly perfected, and a variety of civilian social insurance policies have increased coverage to 98%. As a result of strong national economic growth, improvements have been made to old-age pensions, minimum wages, urban and rural subsistence allowances, and unemployment insurance. The incomes of low-income earners have been constantly improved. Educational equality and the balanced development of compulsory education have been promoted, as have medical and health system reform. The construction of a housing guarantee system has been accelerated so as to help low-income earners improve their living conditions.[2]

Column 3-2 Project 4050

Project '4050' is an essential measure taken by Shanghai municipal government for the purpose of promoting the employment of destitute groups through the operation mechanism of marketization and socialization, aiming to customize the employment positions for destitute women over 40 years old and men over 50 years old. The government provides a 'one package' service in terms of enterprise training, policy consultation, business start-up guidance, reduction and exemption of taxes, and small-sum guaranteed loans. These measures are termed by the United Nation's International Labor Organization as the 'Shanghai model' with regard to 'irregular employment and the elimination of urban poverty'.

2. Reinforcing and innovating social administration on the basis of population management

Shanghai takes the lead in the exploration of the full-coverage administration of 'actual population and actual houses', collecting information on the actual number of people and houses in the whole city and establishing a population information system shared by the whole city, which lays the elementary foundation for the reinforcement of social administration. On the basis of the philosophy of 'integrating administration into service', and in accordance with the system of 'residence permits', a fundamental public service system is

---

[2] Han Zheng. *The Exploration and Practice of Reinforcing and Innovating Shanghai's Social Administration.* Party Building Research, 2011 (4)

established for those coming to live in Shanghai. As long as those coming to live in Shanghai hold a residence permit, they are entitled to public services in areas such as employment. On July 1, 2013, Shanghai implemented *Shanghai Residence Permit Administration Regulations*, becoming the first city in China to adopt a residence permit point accumulation system for administering those people who live in Shanghai but without registered permanent residence. After the implementation of the new regulations, more common laborers have been entitled to more public services depending upon their professional skills and the length of time they have paid social security, and in the meantime the number of their children who join them to live in Shanghai has also risen.

> **Column 3-3 The implementation of Shanghai Residence Permit Administration Regulations and supportive documents**
>
> *Shanghai Residence Permit Administration Regulations* were released on June 19, 2013 and the supporting *Trial Regulations of Shanghai Residence Permit Point-accumulation Administration System* and *Implementation Regulations of Applying for a Shanghai Residence Permit* were officially implemented on July 1. According to the regulations, permit holders will be 'graded' on the basis of factors such as age, educational background and professional title. Those who gain 120 points could enjoy some corresponding public services, including education opportunities for their children, social security, application for certain certificates and licenses, housing, public health and family planning. The indicator system of point-accumulation is composed of an elementary indicator, bonus point indicator, point deduction indicator and one-vote veto indicator, which means that the children of those with 120 points are allowed to take the senior high school entrance examination and college entrance examination in Shanghai.

In the meantime, in order to respond to the guidelines of 'strict control over the population of extra-large cities' put forward in *Decision of the Central Committee of the CPC on Some Key Issues of Comprehensively Deepening Reform*, which was passed in the third plenary session of the 18th Central Committee of the CPC, and in response to the increasingly pressing problems of population size and resource constraints, Shanghai has adhered to the rule of legally stabilizing employment residence, so as to reinforce population service administration, and strictly implementing the residence permit system based on the points system. Shanghai has also taken comprehensive measures to strictly control its population size, such as adjusting the industrial structure, perfecting public policies, removing illegally constructed buildings and fixing group-oriented leasing.

3. Reinforcing and innovating social administration under the framework of hierarchical management

Since 1996, Shanghai has taken the lead in carrying out city administration system reform, implementing the new administration system of 'two-level governments, three-level administration, four-level network' (the two-level governments of the municipal government and the district government, the three-level administration of the city, district and sub-district, the four-level network of the city, district, sub-district and neighborhood committee), transferring the focus of city administration downward, reinforcing the comprehensive administration function of the sub-district community and pushing the community to the frontline of city administration. Under such a model, the focus of city administration is gradually transferring downward, and the sub-district is granted some powers such as getting involved in the planning of some districts, hierarchical management administrative authority, comprehensive coordinating authority and administrative authority. The sub-district has more than 150 work assignment items, which cover all the functions of a regional government, while the neighborhood committee plays an important role in community autonomy.

> **Column 3-4 What is the community neighborhood committee?**
>
> The community neighborhood committee is an autonomous organization of town residents, playing a similar role to the village committee in a rural district, with the serving subjects mainly being non-agricultural residents in cities and towns. According to the organization law of a neighborhood committee, the community neighborhood committee is a grassroots autonomous mass organization through which residents may carry out self-administration, self-education and self-service, managing public affairs within the community on behalf of community members.

In the past decade, Shanghai has explored and innovated the leading mechanism of the community party organizations, forming full-coverage organizations and a working system. On the one hand, in the light of the party organization administration and institutional administration procedure, the sub-district party working committee is revoked while the community (sub-district) party working committee is established, shouldering overall responsibility for regional and societal affairs, and in the interest of the masses and public welfare. In addition, the sub-district exercises dual leadership and dual administration to agencies of district-level functional departments. On the other hand, on the basis of the requirement of 'three lines', 'one group and two committees' are established, comprising the party group of the administrative organization, the comprehensive party committee of the community, and the party committee of the residential area. The setting up of the party group of the administrative organization promotes the role of the community (sub-district) party working committee and the office in exercising dual administration and work collaboration with the agencies of district-level functional departments, facilitating the task of better serving the masses.

4. Reinforcing social administration by means of grassroots innovation

In recent years, Shanghai municipal government has been promoting the transformation of the social administration mode. Previously, the government took exclusive authority over administration and ignored the participation of multiple parties. Today, the mode has changed, with the government now taking a leadership role and multiple parties in society playing an important role. The purpose is to vigorously improve the capability of social organizations to develop themselves and serve society, to fully encourage the public to participate in public welfare activities and social public affairs, and to promote community co-regulation at sub-district level so as to enhance and innovate social administration by means of grassroots initiation.

Since Shanghai issued a regulation to remove street vendors in May 2007, all the districts have positively tried establishing 'evacuation points' for them. Pudong New District established 68 dredging points in 13 downtown sub-districts, giving priority to street vendors providing convenience products and services such as groceries and breakfast, so as to satisfy the living needs of local citizens. In the meantime, the vendors allowed to conduct business in the dredging points are supposed to obey the rules, which cover the following: vendors must not affect the traffic; they shall not create noise that disturbs residents; and no oil fumes are allowed. The evacuation points are administered by a specially-assigned person who formulates the business scope, operating time and line of business. Several measures, such as distributing uniform mobile carts, issuing identity cards, and signing letters of commitment, are taken to ensure that vendors are classified correctly and managed on a regular basis, which eases the problem of erecting booths without regulation. From the second half of 2009, Minhang district started to take some innovative social administration measures. Departments in the district cooperated with each other in terms of urban comprehensive administration, establishing a three-level administration network involving the district, sub-district and village committee, and integrating various administrative resources. As a result, government functional departments, via the information platform, are able to coordinate and link service, administration and law enforcement, and effectively connect daily administration and emergency administration. The big linkage mechanism is based on services relating to people's livelihoods and solving problems at the outset, designed to instantly accept, discover and solve all issues in urban administration, so that the needs concerning people's livelihoods and hidden conflicts could be dealt with quickly at the grassroots level. Therefore, residents in a district may enjoy the positive results of big linkage reform such as convenient services, orderly administration and a harmonious society, in addition to receiving high-quality services from the government and the fruits of social development. In the same year, the general party branch and village committee of Lianqun village in Jiading district initiated a pilot social administration and service scheme, and they collected information on the floating population by means of regular checks, implementing spontaneous grassroots social administration and service pattern, which falls into the dynamic administration. Within the administrative area of the village, all duties pertinent to community safety are integrated, such as the maintenance of stability, postal and telecoms services, judicial conciliation, legal publicity, administration and information collection of the floating population, public security, co-administration of the city's appearance and safe production. Such duties are conducted by the 'five in one' integrated administration station, which represents grassroots work and promotes the integration of ethnic groups and the restoration of humanity.

5. Reinforming and innovating social administration by taking public participation as the core

The report of the 18th National Congress of the CPC pointed out that the establishment of a social administration system should be accelerated, in which the party committee takes a leadership role, the government takes responsibility, civilian organizations coordinate and cooperate, the public participate, and the law is enforced to guarantee the running of society. The first priority is to smooth administrative relations at the grassroots level. A series of documents needed to be worked out; *Regulations of Residence Real*

Estate Management should be revised; and relations between the neighborhood committee, real estate committee and real estate company should be put in order. It should also be made clear that the real estate committee carry out activities under the supervision of the neighborhood committee, and the neighborhood committee reinforces administration in terms of supervising the candidates of the real estate committee, monitoring the employment of the maintenance fund and employing the real estate company. The second priority is to strengthen the autonomous capability of the neighborhood committee. More than 3,000 neighborhood directors in the whole city are gathered to receive training; the personnel structure of the neighborhood committee is optimized; retired party leaders are motivated to participate in the election of neighborhood committees; and local college graduates are encouraged to find employment in neighborhood committees through the legal process. The third priority is to widely carry out democratic autonomous practice at the grassroots level. More than 95% of neighborhood committees across the whole city have established a system of hearing conference (similar to a judicial trial), coordinating conference and evaluating conference, so that the masses can take care of their own affairs. On the basis of implementing these 'three conferences', the grassroots is encouraged to take advantage of local conditions to carry out democratic autonomy, and to improve neighborhood committee functions such as democratic election, democratic administration, democratic policy making and democratic supervision.

Wuliqiao community (sub-district) in Shanghai Huangpu district, guided by the party construction of the community, focuses on the job of serving the masses and actively innovates the working mechanism, coordinating and integrating, relieving and solving, constructing a harmonious community relationship, constantly improving social administration in which the party committee is in charge, the government is responsible, society cooperates and the public participate. As a result, social administration is extended from the simple maintenance of public security to joint social construction and administration. Grassroots democratic autonomy is widely implemented, which is focused on the 'three conferences' system and supported by the public announcement system, responsibility system and commitment system. Other mechanisms are also explored, such as multi-round hearings, the contractualization of practical projects, and the socialized assessment of property management, which along with the further improvement of the systems for civilization pledges and the postal and telecoms agencies, grassroots democratic construction in the community can be promoted. As a result, the opinions of the masses can be widely collected; responsibilities can be fulfilled more efficiently; mass supervision can be carried out more forcefully; and some common disputes can be addressed effectively.

6. Improving the modernization of social administration with the information network

Since the mid-1990s, Shanghai has taken advantage of the development opportunity of global informatization and has always taken informatization as the strategy to cover overall modernism construction. The ninth five-year plan focuses on infrastructure, with an emphasis placed on the construction of information infrastructure; the 10th five-year plan focuses on breakthrough, promoting the rapid development of the information industry and the application of information technology; the 11th five-year plan takes as the main focus 'promoting the innovation of information technology and deepening the application of information technology', promoting in all directions the construction of informatization.

After more than 10 years of work, Shanghai has accomplished all the tasks in the construction of informatization, and the overall informatization level continues to take a lead domestically, with some of the indicators reaching the level of developed countries. Various benefits of information technology innovation have been put into application, and great progress has been achieved in improving social administration by taking advantage of networks. The first is that the basic network has been formed. In response to the national requirement that a uniform electronic government affairs network should be built, Shanghai has established an electronic government affairs network covering the municipal, district and sub-district level, with a utilization rate of 26.1%. Some 81.8% of Shanghai netizens frequently visit government websites to check information, and the network has gradually become a platform for all levels of government to keep the public informed of government affairs. The second benefit is that the function of using networks to guide public opinion has been reinforced. All levels of government in Shanghai attach great importance to public opinion, and the dominant discourse power of internet media is growing in influence. Governments at all levels release various social administration information via the internet, and in addition, many government officials express their opinions through microblogs, leading public opinion in a favorable way, according to a survey by a research group. The third benefit is that much importance is attached to social conditions and public opinion reflected in the virtual network. Public opinion in the network is drawing unprecedented attention, for the network is the means for the government at all levels to know about public opinion; some officials even communicate directly with netizens on the internet to discuss social administration affairs and give timely responses to questions raised by netizens. Email addresses and telephone numbers are posted on government websites so that citizens can easily report problems in government work. Networks are becoming the bridge of communication between Shanghai governments at all levels and citizens. The fourth benefit is that urban grid administration is universally applied in urban areas across the whole city. A set of standardized administration processes has been set up, which is meant to 'be proactive and deal with problems without delay', and therefore digitalized urban administration has reached a new stage.

> **Column 3-5 What is grid administration?**
>
> Grid administration involves dividing an urban administrative area into unit grids (generally one community falls into one grid or is divided into several grids), and then implementing a detailed, informatized and dynamic social service administration by taking people, places, properties, the affairs and organizations into the grid. Grid administration is characterized by the effective integration of party committee and government with various social forces and resources such as communities, villages, non-governmental organizations and volunteers, which both reinforces grassroots governing capability and governing foundation, and represents an elementary but significant innovation of strengthening social administration. Grid administration contributes to the establishment and improvement of the social administration service mechanism on a regular basis, distinguished by the timely discovery of problems, orderly coordination, proper disposal, effective supervision, fulfilled responsibility and adequate service. With such a mechanism, the social service administrative force is delegated, with responsibilities clarified and resources integrated, and the operation is highly efficient, thereby improving the government's administrative level and emergency capacity through the realization of 'zero distance' of social service, 'full coverage' of social administration and 'total response' to people's appeals.

II. Actively developing community construction

Community construction is a new term coined after China's reform and opening up. The variety of community construction and community service measures aimed at specific social issues and social groups are the major means taken by countries to amend the social body and resolve social issues.

This may include, for example, early community public service and sub-district construction in the US, urban and community reconstruction of major European countries such as the UK, France and Germany after two destructive world wars, and Canada's recent solution to the problems of laid-off workers and finding employment again by means of community service. In 30 years since the start of reform and opening up, great changes have taken place in China's economic society and city construction, and community construction has featured on the agenda. In recent years, Shanghai municipal government has attached great importance to community construction and has achieved conspicuous achievements, which may be illustrated as follows.

1. Establishing an effective model of resident autonomy

On the level of neighborhood committee, Shanghai implements the autonomy model, by which the party organization takes a leadership role, and the neighborhood committee, real estate committee, real estate company and social work station act jointly (sometimes known as 'one horse leading four wheels'). Such an administrative model is characterized by the leading role of the party organization, the major role of the neighborhood committee and real estate committee, the main body role of residents, and the initiative role of the real estate company and social work station. To explore and implement community autonomy, a community committee is established in some communities so that the community problems can be addressed; the benefits for many parties can be coordinated and grassroots democracy can be realized. Yinxing sub-district of Yangpu district established the community representative congress system in 2006, and the representatives come not only from the neighborhood, but also from work units in the community, and four specialized committees are set up, covering urban area administration, social development, social security and public security. The first community committee in Shanghai – the Community Committee of Quyang community in Hongkou district – was established in March 2009, and is composed of the sub-district office and work units within the administrative region such as the Lansheng hotel, Yueyang hospital and Tonghua Municipal Engineering Company. The committee consists of another five specialized committees covering economic development, city construction, social undertakings of science, education, culture, health and sports, social security, and the NPC, CPPCC, workers' council, youth council and women's council.

2. Promoting the development of community service

In 1989, Shanghai initiated a pilot in Dapuqiao sub-district in Luwan district and established the first sub-district community service center in the whole city. Since 1992, with direct encouragement from the municipal party committee and the municipal government, community service in Shanghai has been categorized as a practical project by Shanghai municipal government, and it is required that a community service center should be established in 50% of sub-districts and a community volunteer service should be established in 1,000 neighborhood committees, which is a sign that the construction of the community service center has been officially listed on the agenda. In 1997, Shanghai initiated the informatization of Shanghai community services, and Shanghai community service center was officially established. Thereafter, sub-districts began to build their own community service center, or to renovate public service facilities into community service centers. By 2000, 95% of sub-districts had established a community service center, with a community service hotline set up in the area under administration, and 85% of the neighborhood committees established a community service center. In 2002, a new pattern of 'three nets make a joint move' eventually took shape in Shanghai, which means 'one community service center, 14 district community service centers and 116 sub-district community service centers'. In 2006, some districts and counties initiated a pilot project to construct community affairs acceptance centers, community health service centers and community cultural activity centers.

On the basis of Shanghai's community service experience, the community service center includes more than 100 service items in eight categories. The first category is life services, aimed at the daily lives of community residents and usually known as 'convenience and benefit services', which mainly covers maintenance and housekeeping services. The second is the irregular employment service provided for all residents, including skills training, community barbershops, community tailor's shops, community afforestation, house cleaning, collection of public utility fees, funeral and internment services, household maintenance services and neighborhood bicycle shed management. The third category is public security services, including community security patrol, dispute resolution, education of troubled adolescents, and help and education for those released from prison. The fourth is cultural and sport services, covering sport activities, a variety of skill and cultural training, and classes on hobbies. The fifth is the service provided to special groups, mainly targeted at the old, disabled and families in financial difficulty; the service covers all aspects of their lives. The sixth category is intermediary services such as real estate, insurance and employment agencies. The seventh is medical services such as community hospitals and private clinics, and the eighth is consultation services such as psychological counseling, health consultation and legal services, which fall into two categories of information consultation and commercial service consultation.

3. Promoting the development of social organizations

Shanghai has always attached great importance to social organizations. In recent years, centering on the requirements of constructing an extra-large international metropolis, Shanghai has taken the lead in exploring new paths and new measures to foster and develop social organizations, striving to optimize the development environment of social organizations and promote the sound growth of social organizations. Currently, the frame system of the development and administration of social organizations has been formed, which is coherent with the development of economic society, justifiable in structure, orderly and forceful in supervision, and democratic and self-disciplined. Therefore, the construction of social organizations in Shanghai leads the country.

Up to the end of 2012, there were 10,745 social organizations registered in civil affairs departments, and in Shanghai there are as many as 7.6 social organizations for every 10,000 registered Shanghai residents, more than twice the national average. Shanghai social organizations have some interesting features, and in general are healthy and orderly. From 2006 to 2012, the average annual growth rate of social organizations in the city was 5.3%, and compared with 2004, the number of employees increased from 125,000 to 185,000. Social organizations are becoming more and more involved in international exchange and cooperation, and by the end of 2012, there were 35 registered social organizations concerning foreign affairs, involving 12 countries and regions. Their public product supply capacity continues to grow and has become an important supplement of social undertakings. Those organizations also play a more conspicuous role of participation in social administration, playing a positive role in the placement of demobilized army officers, managing services to the transient population, dealing with problems related to household demolition and relocation, and alleviating tensions between doctors and patients. In addition, the social influence of network associations has become more and more far-reaching.

Shanghai's experiences in promoting the development of social organizations are mainly as follows:

(1) Buying more services from social organizations and offering developing resources and space to non-government organizations. Since 2000, Shanghai has explored the purchase of social organization services by the government in the field of providing for the elderly. In 2012, Shanghai Municipal Finance Bureau issued *Shanghai Interim Procedures of Budget Control for the Municipal Government to Purchase Public Services* and *Shanghai Item Directory of Municipal Government Purchasing Public Service (2013)*, thus forming the entire development system for social organizations covering everything from venture capital investment of public welfare to public welfare bidding and tendering, and then further to the institutionalized purchase of public services by the government. Currently, the purchase of social organization services has been popularized in Shanghai governments at all levels. In 2012, the revenue of social organizations from government purchases exceeded Rmb4.5bn, accounting for 15% of the total revenue of Shanghai's social organizations.

(2) Promoting the construction of incubators and fostering the social organization model. Since 2009, Shanghai has established 17 incubators at the city, district and sub-district level, selecting some social organizations that are innovative and up to the social needs to be fostered in incubators, and providing them with support services such as office workplace, financial management, fund raising and project planning.

(3) Enhancing talent and improving the capability of social organizations. Talent in social organizations is taken into the category of 'talent under the administration of the party', and taken into the medium- and long-term plans of talent development, so as to attract talent and stabilize the team. Shanghai exerts considerable efforts to increase the proportion of representatives from social organizations in the party congress and people's congress at all levels in the city, and is committed to increase the number of committee members from social organizations in the people's political consultative conference. More than 700 people from social organizations in the whole city act as representatives or committee members.

(4) Striving to promote the reform of social organizations and explore their sustainable development. In 2002, Shanghai took the lead in implementing the separation of trade associations and government

bodies in terms of 'personnel, agencies, finance and assets'. In 2009, this separation spread to enterprise associations and chambers of commerce. In 2010, Shanghai Municipal People's Congress made revisions to *Shanghai Regulations on Promoting the Development of Trade Associations*, clearly defining important aspects such as direct registration, separation between political administration and associations, the development of personnel professionalization, and the establishment of a resignation mechanism.

(5) Looking to establish a comprehensive service supervision system of social organizations. Civil affairs departments are responsible for formulating the qualifications of social organizations that take over government services, checking a directory of social organizations, taking the services they provide to the government in the annual inspection, assessment and law enforcement system, and participating in the performance appraisal of the government purchasing service from social organizations. The competent functional departments are in charge of purchasing from social organizations, making purchasing budgets, tracking and supervising the service, and checking and evaluating the service once it has been delivered. The auditing and discipline inspection departments are responsible for the auditing and supervision of the capital employed by the government in the purchase of services from social organizations.

4. Promoting the professionalization of social work

Shanghai was one of the first batch of cities on the Chinese mainland to launch social work practice and promote the development of social work talent. In 1993, in response to a call from Ministry of Civil Affairs to develop social work, Shanghai Social Workers' Association was established. This marked the official start of the construction of social work talent in Shanghai. In 2000, Shanghai Social Work Training Center was set up, which to date is the only provincial-level training institution with 'social work' in its name and is sponsored by the government to carry out social work training. On March 16, 2003, Shanghai Personnel Bureau and Shanghai Civil Affairs Bureau formulated and issued *Shanghai Interim Procedures for the Professional Qualification Authentication of Social Workers*, which was the first institutional document in the professional construction of social work in Shanghai. It was also a legal basis for social workers to achieve a professional qualification, and established for the first time the professional term and professional image of 'social workers'. In 2004, Shanghai Civil Affairs Bureau took the lead in setting up a professional social work division, which was put in charge of coordinating the development of social work across the whole city. In 2011, Shanghai Social Workers' Association held its third representative conference, elected new leaders who were mostly social work professionals or educationalists, thus establishing the pattern of putting experts in charge of the association, and making the association operate autonomously. District-level social workers' associations were also set up in the districts of Pudong, Huangpu, Yangpu, Jing'an, Xuhui, Changning, Putuo and Zhabei, which brought about ever-improving capabilities in trade management and service.

The most essential characteristics of Shanghai's social work system can be summarized as 'cooperation between the government and society, the autonomous operation of social organizations and the universal participation of people'. In accordance with the strategy of 'overall design, whole promotion and classified guidance', Shanghai is gradually promoting social work development and social work talent construction in terms of system building, institution construction, talent distribution, field expansion, talent cultivation, and support and guarantee. So far, Shanghai has established the professional status of social workers from the perspective of public policies and has established the agencies of public administration and professional service, as well as associations, and therefore a tripartite social work administration system has taken initial shape, with the three parties being 'the government, service agency and social workers'. The service scope keeps expanding, and the talent pool keeps growing, with support from all aspects enhanced. There are already 16 social education and training institutions in Shanghai, including East China University of Science and Technology, Fudan University, Shanghai University and Shanghai Social Work Training Center. The number of people with various social work professional qualifications in Shanghai is approaching 14,000, and the number of social organizations offering social work services is 115, of which 66 are professional social work agencies where social workers are in the majority. The 66 professional social work agencies include 13 associations at the city, district and sub-district level, one social work training agency, one research and assessment agency and 51 direct service agencies.[3] Therefore, the developing trend of Shanghai social

---

[3] Guo Yundan, Wu Fang. 'The 20-year Development of Shanghai Social Work', *China Social Work* [J], 2012 (11)

work has taken initial shape, in which direct service agencies play the main role and indirect service agencies play a supporting role.

5. Innovating the international community administration pattern

As Shanghai accelerates its pace to building itself into an international metropolis, there are more and more 'international communities' in which the proportion of international residents exceeds 30% and can be as high as 60-80% in Gubei, Lianyang, Biyun and Xintiandi. In these international communities, the traditional organization and working style are unlikely to meet demand due to the differences of those residents in values, religion and customs. Under the leadership of the sub-district party committee, such communities fully stimulate the initiatives of international residents, positively building an internationalized administration platform and thus exploring an innovation path of international community administration, which bears Chinese characteristics. For instance, on August 22, 2007, Hongqiao sub-district in Changning district established the Gubei New Sub-district Committee for the Promotion of Community Construction, inviting representatives of national and international residents, property management companies and community units that show their concern for community construction, to shoulder the work of coordinating public and welfare affairs in the community. Another example is Huaihai Road sub-district in Luwan district (now Huangpu district), which established Xintiandi Consultation and Administration Committee of Resident Affairs, which has European, American, Asian, Australian, African and other foreign branch committees, with residents from 37 countries and regions encouraged to join them to 'take responsibility'.

III. Establishing and perfecting the social security system

Shanghai's traditional social security system is mainly composed of a government guarantee, enterprise guarantee and countryside collective guarantee, thus forming the 'three security nets' that are independent from each other. Government guarantee covers relief, welfare, subsidy, veteran benefits and disaster relief; enterprise guarantee, with the enterprise being the main body and employees and their families being the subjects, includes employment, endowment, occupational injury, medical treatment, fertility, hardship and welfare; countryside collective guarantee, with the countryside collective organizations being the main body and farmers being the subjects, involves cooperative medical services and the supply of necessities for people in extreme difficulties such as 'families entitled to five guarantees'.

> **Column 3-6 Who are entitled to the five guarantees?**
>
> Families entitled to five guarantees, according to the *Regulations of the Five Guarantee Support in the Countryside*, refer to the subjects for whom the five types of guarantees are provided. They mainly comprise the elderly, the disabled and juveniles who lack the capacity to work or earn income, and who have no one legally obliged to support them, or have no supporting capability even with legal supporting obligators. The five guarantees comprise food, clothing, medical care, housing and burial expenses (or nursing expenses for orphans). 'Families entitled to five guarantees' are usually found in China's countryside, and the establishment of such a system is a reflection of both humanism and the consistent principle of the law in our country, which is committed to the protection of the elderly and children.

Since reform and opening up, Shanghai has carried out a series of social security reforms, and in accordance with the principle of 'classification, hierarchy, elementary guarantee and overall coverage', has explored the establishment of a social security system and made particular progress since the beginning of the 1990s.

1. The initial shaping of the social security system conforming to the actual situation in Shanghai

On the basis of the retirement pay pooling in state-owned enterprises that was introduced in 1986, since 1993 Shanghai established a basic endowment insurance system in cities and towns, which combines the social pooling and individual account, expanding the pooling scope to all enterprises and institutions in the city. Thereafter, the insurance systems of unemployment, medical treatment, fertility and occupational injury were set up successively, which contributed to the formation of the 'five-in-one' basic endowment insurance system in cities and towns. Such a system provides a 'baseline' guarantee for suburban farmers not living off the land in terms of their subsistence rights, development rights and guarantee rights, thus improving their competitiveness in terms of non-agricultural employment. The rural social endowment insurance system was stablished in 1996, with the comprehensive insurance system for non-local employees following in 2002 and the town social insurance system in 2003. Since the second half of 2006, those excluded from the basic social insurance system have gradually been included in various insurance types. As a result, Shanghai has primarily formed a social security system matching the development of 'four centers' and its economic status, integrating the urban and rural, and including all types of people.

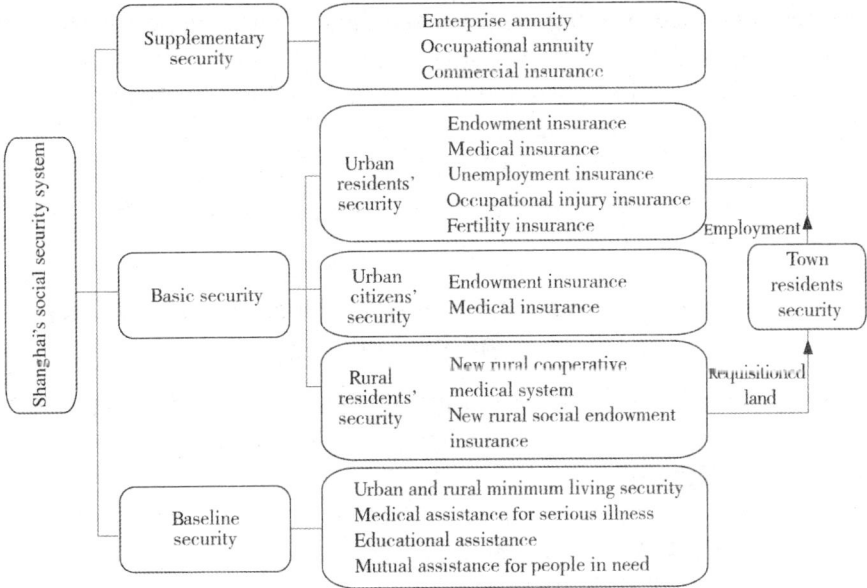

Figure 3-4 Shanghai's social security system

2. The ever-growing coverage of social security

During the '11th five-year plan', Shanghai's social security coverage kept growing. In December 2007, Shanghai issued the operation regulations of basic medical insurance for urban residents, and in December 2008 an endowment guarantee system for the urban elderly was released, which created the full coverage of the endowment and medical insurance systems to all registered citizens. In 2009, foreigners and compatriots from Hong Kong, Macau and Taiwan, as well as local citizens' spouses without local registration, were all taken into the social security system for urban employees, and those suffering from 'occupational injury' were taken into the system of occupational insurance fund. After the implementation of the new *Social Insurance Law* on July 1, 2011, Shanghai municipal government issued a new policy in a document which meant that all employees in Shanghai's urban and rural areas, who had no local household registration, were taken into the social security system for urban employees.

Today, Shanghai has established a medical insurance system characterized by 'three verticals and three horizontals', which means that the basic medical insurance system, supplementary medical insurance system and medical assistance system are taken as the three guarantee horizons, with the basic medical insurance system covering medical insurance for urban employees, medical insurance for urban residents and the new rural cooperative medical system (NCMS). By 2012, the number of insured urban employees reached 13.37m, and that of urban residents 2.55m, with their combined total reaching 15.93m. Such a large total combined with the number of those insured under the NCMS, contributed to the full coverage of the medical insurance system, with the proportion of the registered population receiving insurance exceeding 96%.

3. The constant improvement of the social security system mechanism

To carry out the State Council decision to reform medical treatment and the public health system, Shanghai implemented the 'combination' of socialized medicine and the labor medicare system, and constructed an urban basic medical insurance system that is characterized by 'the combination of social pooling and the individual account'. In addition, some supporting measures were implemented, such as the burden alleviation of medical insurance for vulnerable groups, the labor union mutual assistance guarantee of medical treatment and the medical assistance guarantee for employees. The three-level social security service network covering the city, district (county) and sub-district (town) has been further improved, and the establishment of 261 sub-district and town medical insurance service stations has effectively delegated the provision of medical insurance services. In the whole city, there are 1,400 designated medical insurance stations that are networked, and in every sub-district and town, there is at least one designated community health service agency, one designated retail drugstore and one community medical insurance station, so that citizens can access medical treatment and purchase medicine with a single social security card. The social security cooperative mechanism in the Yangtze River Delta was initiated. Shanghai's labor security administration information system has been constructed, followed by the establishment of government social security websites and the opening of consultation service hotlines, which are new channels of communication with citizens. All social security insurance benefits have been distributed to the masses.

4. Constantly improving the multilayered endowment system

Since the '11th five-year plan', in order to cope with the ever growing aging problem, Shanghai has formulated and improved the '9073' endowment pattern, which means that 90% of the elderly are taken care of by their own families, 7% are supported at home by community services and 3% at nursing homes. These nursing homes are led by the government and society is encouraged to participate, so that they could provide those advanced in age and disabled old people with full-time nursing care. There are different types of nursing institution, such as those built by government, private institutions sponsored by the government and institutions operated completely according to the market principle. When it comes to the 7% of the elderly supported by community endowment services, the main bodies offering such services are specialist community service agencies, daytime service centers for the aged and community service stations providing catering assistance, with the visiting service and daytime service being the main forms and daily life care, rehabilitation nursing and spiritual consolation being the main contents. In addition, by means of enhancing community facilities designed for the elderly (such as barrier-free facilities and activity rooms for the elderly) and expanding the renovation of facilities designed for the elderly in old urban areas (including house renovations for old people in difficulty, pavement renovation in old neighborhoods and the installation of elevators), 90% of old people are encouraged to be taken care of by their own families.

IV. Developing and improving social undertakings

Over the 35 years of reform and opening up, with the rapid growth of the economy, people's living standards have improved conspicuously, and the social undertakings in Shanghai have also developed significantly.

1. The clear growth in public service supply capability

Capability construction is an important sign that social undertakings promote economic development and provide efficient service to the masses. Currently, the cultural contribution to Shanghai's economy is 5.6%, and the educational contribution has reached the level of moderately developed countries. Sporting events, touring, conventions and exhibitions may drive the development of related industries, at a ratio of 1:5. A public cultural system covering urban and rural areas has been established, and the per capita area of public cultural facilities is now 0.18 square meters. A learning-oriented urban framework has taken shape, in which people may learn anytime, anywhere, and thus the average schooling length of the incoming labor force is 14.5 years. Also constructed are public health and basic medical treatment services, which are safe, efficient, convenient and offered equally to all citizens, and an old-age service system that involves 10% of elderly people being entitled to institution-based or home-based endowment services. In addition, fitness facilities and the physical health of citizens have reached the level of moderately developed countries and regions. Apart from efforts to accelerate the development of its own social undertakings, Shanghai also plays a positive role in serving the whole country and the Yangtze River Delta region in particular. Higher education, vocational education and various types of training are offered to set up a platform for the Yangtze River Delta and the country, exporting more than 50,000 talented individuals to other cities each year, and putting on training courses that cater to more than 1m people. Medical treatment services are offered to meet the needs of local citizens, as well as to approximately one third of all people in the Yangtze River Delta region and the whole country.

2. Gradual perfection of the social undertakings layout structure

Rational layout is the important foundation for social undertakings to serve people. In recent years, the layout of some major cultural facilities has been further optimized, and some construction projects have been accomplished or launched, such as the Shanghai History Museum, Shanghai Natural History Museum, Shanghai Maritime Museum and Shanghai World Expo Museum. The layout readjustment of colleges and universities, as well as disciplines and subjects, has been accelerated, and the number of key disciplines in universities increased by 10%, so as to promote the shift of high-quality elementary education resources to suburban areas and immigrant population communities. In outer suburbs such as Chongming, Jinshan and Fengxian, as well as in Pudong, tertiary hospitals or branches have been set up, which is the result of partner assistance and trusteeship. The 'three centers' in communities (cultural activity, health services and general affairs) have been implemented in all urban and rural areas. Therefore, citizens can reach a medical treatment station within a 15-minute-walk, and a public entertainment and sports facility within a 10-minute-walk.

Column 3-7 The spatial layout adjustment of Shanghai's universities in the 21st century

With the support of the Ministry of Education, and marked by the construction of Songjiang University Park in June 2000, Shanghai has initiated a new round of university spatial layout adjustment and the construction of new campuses. The original overall layout plan was '2+2+X', with the first '2' referring to the two university agglomerations centered on key universities in the south and the north. In the north, there is the Yangpu knowledge innovation area centered on Fudan University, together with 11 universities such as Tongji and Shanghai University of Finance and Economics, 22 national key laboratories and more than 100 scientific research institutions. In the south, in Minhang Zizhu Scientific Park with Shanghai Jiaotong University as the core, are clustered universities such as East China Normal University. The second '2' refers to Songjiang University Park in the west, including seven universities such as Shanghai International Studies University, Donghua University and East China University of Political Science and Law. In the east is Nanhui Science and Education Park, in which there are four universities, two private schools and one independent institute. 'X' refers to the construction of universities partly dependent on industry development zones and industrial parks. The new campus of Tongji University built in Jiading Anting has become the key technical R&D platform of Jiading's automobile industry, as well as the base of talent training. Shanghai University of Traditional Chinese Medicine and Fudan Microelectronics Research Institute have been transferred to Pudong, participating in the development of high-tech industries centered on microelectronics, software, and biological medicine. In 2005, Shanghai municipal party committee and Shanghai municipal government decided to build two more university parks in Fengxian district and Lingang New Town, with the layout structure extended as '2+2+2+X'. Fengxian university park and the supporting community cover an area of about 10 square kilometers, with the settlement of East China University of Science and Technology, Shanghai Normal University, Shanghai Institute of Technology and Shanghai Business School. In the science and education innovation park of Lingang New Town, there are Shanghai Ocean University, Shanghai Maritime University and Shanghai Dianji University. The large-scale layout adjustment and the new campus construction in Shanghai provide the basic conditions for an increase in enrollment, and form the new mechanism of 'three-zone linkage' (university campuses, science and technology parks, and urban areas) and with the 'three zone integration; development in linkage', Shanghai succeeds in taking a new path of urban development driven by universities, and university development with the participation of the city proper. (Party Committee of Shanghai Municipal Science and Education Office: 'Promoting Educational System Reform, Implementing University Layout Adjustment", *Jiefang Daily*, December 26, 2008.)

3. The ever-increasing financial input

A high government input is the fundamental guarantee of the rapid development of social undertakings. Since 2002, governments at all levels have increased year by year the social undertaking input, with the educational input continuing to increase, while the input in health, culture and physical education has kept pace with fiscal recurring income, with the fund of community prevention and health care amounting to Rmb40 per person per year. The new financial resources show a priority for the suburbs and grassroots, and 70% of the new fund of education and health is invested in the countryside in the outer suburbs.

4. Further deepening system reform

System and mechanism innovation is the fundamental impetus boosting the sound development of the social undertakings. In recent years, Shanghai has vigorously implemented comprehensive educational reform, and gradually carried forward the independent recruitment of students by universities, putting into practice the policy of 'two exemptions and one subsidy' so as to further balance urban and rural educational development. The reform of medical treatment and public health has deepened, with the basic medical security system gradually perfected and the essential medicine system established. There have been conspicuous achievements in the comprehensive reform of community health services, and with the administrative separation between revenue and expenditure, and the implementation of the prospective payment system in the total amount of medical insurance, community clinics could assume their important responsibilities.

Though social undertakings in Shanghai have been fruitful, there is still a long way to go before reaching the great target of constructing 'four centers'. It is essential that Shanghai further promotes the development of social undertakings, in line with the trend of economic globalization and in the great pattern of national development.

V. Enhancing integrated population administration

Shanghai, as one of the most vigorous cities in China and relying on its favorable regional advantage and open and prosperous economic development, attracts a floating population from all parts of the country. It has become one of the largest places in China for the agglomeration of a floating population. Those who come to work in Shanghai play a vital role in promoting urban construction, social development, environmental improvement, relieving the aging process of Shanghai's urban laborers and making up for the negative growth of the workforce with a Shanghai residency. Therefore, they are gradually becoming an important force in urban economic construction. However, the influx of a large number of people who come to work in Shanghai, especially those drawn by the prospect of welfare payments, has put a great strain on Shanghai's resources and presents a challenge to its comprehensive service and administration. As a result, Shanghai faces a major challenge in how to enhance the comprehensive administration of the population.

1. Establishing the scientific comprehensive population administration system

Shanghai has municipal leading groups to control its population, including ones that address family planning and the migrant population. In May 2003, Shanghai established a municipal leading group for comprehensive population regulation, which is in charge of coordinating, guiding and supervising related departments to carry out population services and administration. Shanghai also enhanced the leadership and coordination of comprehensive population regulation and administration in the whole city, and tentatively established a population administration system of 'comprehensive coordination at the municipal level, comprehensive administration at the district level and concrete implementation in the community', forming a comprehensive population regulation mechanism and related policies, and further improving the efficiency and level of comprehensive population administration.

2. Constructing the full-coverage administrative mechanism of 'two actuals'

With an ever-growing floating population and a marked change in age profile, revolutionary changes are also taking place in the requirements for administering Shanghai. Since 2006, Hongkou district has taken the lead in promoting information collection of the actual population, making an overall survey of the basic situation of the registered population, floating population and foreign population, and constructing a three-level population information data platform covering the whole district, sub-districts and neighborhood committees. On the basis of the pilot, in September 2007, Shanghai municipal government initiated the construction of 'Shanghai Actual Population Information Administration System', and listed it among the 54 major projects of the city. The 'two actuals' refer to comprehensively collecting information on the actual residences and comprehensively collecting information on the actual resident population, including the registered population (separating household registration and actual residence), floating population and foreign population. By means of the full-coverage administration of 'actual population and actual residences', better and more accurate information could be compiled on the actual population, which provides evidence for the reinforcement of city plans and regulations, and the rational allocation of resources. By the end of 2009, Shanghai had essentially accomplished the full-coverage administration of 'two actuals', establishing population information system networking for the whole city, covering villages and towns, sub-districts, all functional departments, the labor force market and talent market. Such a system realizes the integration and sharing of information resources in terms of population, employment, distribution and social security, reinforces the dynamic monitoring and analytical research of population information, and provides technical conditions for leadership decision-making, administration of functional departments and life services to its citizens.

3. Exploring and implementing the administrative regulation of residence permit points

With the development of the social economy and the acceleration of the urbanization process, the proportion of those who come to live and work in Shanghai as a proportion of the city's total population will continue to grow, and government agencies will feel increasing pressure in terms of public administration and service. Since issuing *Temporary Provisions of Shanghai Residence Permit* in August 2004, the residence permit system has become the basic system of social administration and public service in Shanghai, and has become an important support in reinforcing comprehensive population control and administration. Such a system is going through gradual change from static to dynamic administration, and with regard to administrative means, importance is attached to the role of the benefit orientation mechanism, and the supporting reform of social policies is also implemented. *Tentative Regulations of Shanghai Residence Permit Point-accumulation Administration* were implemented on July 1, 2013. Through popularizing the residence permit point-accumulation administration system, and in accordance with the principles by which rights should match obligations and taking should correspond with giving, the relationship between the residence booklet and residence permit, and the relationship between the registered population and the permanent population without residence booklets could both be gradually straightened out. Such a measure could not only guarantee the legitimate interests of those coming to live and work in Shanghai and normalize population service and administration in order to help those coming in to Shanghai better integrate, but also contribute to improving government services and administration, and promoting the harmonious development of the city's economy, society, resources and environment.

Chapter 4

The Development and Prosperity of Shanghai Culture

As a result of its rapid development during the '11th five-year plan', Shanghai culture has made conspicuous achievements. It has led the country in terms of reforming the cultural system, constructing a public culture service system, developing an emerging cultural industry and promoting international cultural exchange. As a result, the soft power of urban culture has been greatly upgraded, boosting the transformation of urban development. However, there are still many shortcomings in the process of Shanghai's cultural construction, and there remains a large gap between Shanghai and international metropolises such as New York, London and Paris in aspects of deep-seated constraints of the cultural system, the development impetus of the creative industry, the identity of city spirit and the participation of all citizens. This chapter analyses some problems in the field of culture, focusing on the target, idea and path of Shanghai's cultural construction, and the cultural industry, public culture service and urban tourism development as well.

I. Reforming and improving the cultural system mechanism

Since the 1980s, Shanghai has kept reforming the cultural system and fostered a number of influential national cultural market participants, establishing a new type of cultural system that matches the socialist spiritual civilization and market economy, and which is 'led by the party committee, supervised by the government, industrial self-discipline, and legally operated by enterprises and public cultural institutions'.

1. The basic idea of cultural system reform

(1) Deepening the internal reform of public cultural institutions. Institutions such as public libraries, museums, cultural centers, science and technology

museums, mass art centers and art galleries are categorized as non-profit public cultural institutions, providing public cultural services to the masses. As for key news media such as party newspapers and journals, radio and television stations, news agencies, newspapers and journals focusing on current affairs, the public institution system still prevails, with internal reform deepened. The minority of art troupes bearing national characteristics and reaching the state standard, though endowed with some for-profit element, are still not qualified enough to be completely market-oriented. Such troupes are supposed to be under an enterprise-style management system without changing their nature of being public institutions, and they are encouraged to constantly grow and develop while serving the masses and the market.

(2) Promoting the transformation of for-profit cultural institutions into enterprises. Such a transformation is the key element of cultural system reform. For-profit cultural institutions, including publishing houses, Xinhua bookstore, film studios, movie theaters, television producers, cultural intermediaries and some entertainment agencies, will be gradually transformed into enterprises with the establishment of a modern enterprise system. Separation between publicity and operation is implemented in the key new media, with operational businesses stripped off from assets so as to carry out 'enterprization' and 'marketization'. When it comes to party newspapers and journals, their means of printing and distribution has been propelled by means of establishing independent companies to expand the market. As for radio and television stations, the separation of producing and broadcasting is promoted, with the production of TV programs made independent. Non-current affairs newspapers and journals, and news websites should be turned gradually into enterprises. As for state-owned entertainment troupes, which specialize in song and dance, acrobatics, Chinese folk art and local opera, explorations will be made to have some of them transformed into enterprises, for they operate in a comparatively mature market.

(3) Reinforcing the construction of the public cultural service system. Under the principle of being non-profit, equal and fair, fundamental and convenient, and in accordance with the idea of government orientation, social participation, and mass construction and mass sharing, the urban and rural masses should be provided with basic public cultural services such as watching television, listening to the radio, reading books and newspapers, public cultural services, and participation in mass cultural activities. Through promoting the construction of public cultural infrastructure and public service, and the innovation of the operation

mechanism of public cultural service, a stable input guarantee mechanism can be established, and the resource allocation of grassroots public culture optimized, with the employment and administration of public cultural facilities reinforced. In the meantime, the relationship between the government, the market and society is properly handled, with importance attached to the role of the market and society in the supply of public cultural services.

(4) Promoting the strategic adjustment of the cultural creation industry. Industrial planning is reinforced and industrial layout is perfected. Through improving the concentration of the cultural industry, and by accelerating mergers and reorganizations of cultural enterprises, a number of backbone cultural enterprises and strategic investors can be developed. Investment and financing channels are broadened, and support is given to qualified cultural enterprises to be listed. Non-public capital investment is also encouraged in the cultural industry, where policies allow. Modern technology and production techniques are fully employed to accelerate the upgrading of cultural industries. The traditional cultural industry encourages integration with the internet and other new technologies to foster new types of operation.

(5) Fostering a modern cultural market system. A modern cultural market system is constructed that is unified and open, competitive and orderly. Cultural intermediaries should play their roles fully in leading trade organizations to fulfil the functions of coordination, supervision, safeguarding rights and services, so as to promote the globalization of cultural enterprises, and motivate the integration of cultural products and services into mainstream societies overseas.

(6) Further transforming government functions. Administrative departments should be separated from for-profit public institutions, in order to separate government functions from enterprise management. The comprehensive reform of administrative law enforcement in the cultural market should be promoted, and the current administrative law enforcement team in fields such as cultural radio, film and television, and press and publications should be integrated to establish a unified law enforcement institution.

2. Main measures of cultural system reform

The first measure is to accelerate system construction. From 2003 to 2006, Shanghai carried out pilot reforms in the two aspects of building a new cultural administration system, and the shaping of the new main body of the cultural market. At the macroscopic level, the 'Shanghai model'[1] concerning state-owned assets supervision in the cultural field was established, as was the public welfare cultural fund (Shanghai Cultural Development Foundation),[2] operational cultural industry investment (Shanghai Jingwen Investment),[3] the delivery system of public cultural services and the law enforcement system of the cultural market; the establishment of 14 cultural trade associations was also promoted. At the microscopic level, Shanghai accomplished the integrative system transformation of Century Publishing Group, Shanghai Literature and Art Publishing Group, and Film Group, and accomplished the shareholding reform and back-door listing of Xinhua Press Circulation Group. It also explored the operation mode of non-profit entertainment agencies by taking Shanghai Grand Theatre Arts Center as the example. These significant reform measures have sketched a new framework of cultural development.

The second measure is to enhance platform construction. From 2006 to 2008, with the target of constructing the 'three systems' (public cultural service system, cultural industry system and cultural market system), Shanghai dispatched cultural and art instructors to communities, planning and building 22 key public cultural facilities with a total investment of Rmb7.33bn. Shanghai vigorously promotes public platform construction of the cultural industry, and has established an international trading platform of cultural services, an investment and financing platform of cultural industries, a trading platform of cultural property rights, and Zhangjiang national digital press base and animation valley.[4] Shanghai for-profit publishers have been transformed into enterprises on schedule. The production of radio and television programs has been separated from broadcasting, and Radio and Television Shanghai and Shanghai Orient Media Group have been established. The integration of radio and television transmission networks has been accomplished, as well as the system reform of state-owned art troupes attached to either the city or county. The system transformation reform of the first batch of non-current affairs newspapers

---

[1] Shanghai established the supervision and administration office of state-owned assets in the cultural field. http://hxd.wenming.cn/whtzgg/2009-10/27/content_62610.htm

[2] www.shcdf.org

[3] www.jinwin.com.cn

[4] www.animation-park.com/

and journals has been completed, and the first private investment fund of cultural industries in China has been established – China Media Capital. In addition, Shanghai has completed the system transformation of county cinemas, and reorganized Century Publishing Group and the Literature and Art Publishing Group.

The third measure is to accelerate the system transformation of cultural institutions into enterprises. Through the promotion of efficiency, order, support and devolution, Shanghai has completed the system transformation of all for-profit cultural institutions. From 2004 to May 2012, as part of the cultural system reform, as many as 54 institutional units were revoked in the municipal propaganda and cultural system, and institutional transformation was accomplished in film production, publication and distribution, printing, broadcasting and TV production, resulting in a number of backbone state-owned cultural enterprises.[5] In the area of literature and art troupes, for example, institutional reforms have been carried out on the basis of 'three types' in 16 municipal literature and art troupes. The institutional system is kept in six municipal literature and art troupes: Shanghai Jinju Company, Shanghai Kunqu Opera Troupe, Shanghai Symphony Orchestra, Shanghai Ballet, Shanghai Opera House and Shanghai Chinese Orchestra. The institutional system has also been kept in Shanghai Yue Opera House, Shanghai Hu Opera House, Shanghai Huai Opera Troupe and Shanghai Pingtan Troupe, for they are regarded as local opera troupes with national-level intangible cultural heritage, and so have been re-established as 'public welfare reserve and heritage institutions'. This has left six troupes to be transformed as enterprises: Shanghai Acrobatic Troupe, Shanghai Dramatic Arts Center, Shanghai Farce Troupe, Shanghai Dance Theatre, Shanghai Light Music Orchestra and Shanghai Puppet Theatre. Due to the appropriate plan and layout, a new creation-type structure has been formed, in which the performance culture is developed by means of multiple systems, and the troupes are supported with a variety of approaches. In addition, 11 literature and art troupes at district or county level have experienced institutional reform, which contributes to the improved development of Shanghai's cultural and performing industries. In 2013, the merger of the two press groups, Wenxin Group and Jiefang Daily, laid the foundation for the further development of Shanghai cultural industries.

---

[5] Wu Bin. Increase of Impetus and Growth of Vitality: the Accomplishment of Phasal Task of Shanghai Cultural System Reform [N], *Jiefang Daily*, November 13, 2012

> **Column 4-1 Merger of two press groups in Shanghai**
>
> Shanghai United Media Group was established in October 2013 through the merger of Wenhui-Xinmin United Press Group and Jiefang Daily Group. The two groups own more than 10 newspapers and enterprises, including *Xinmin Evening News*, which enjoys the longest history in China, and *Jiefang Daily*, which used to be the official organ of the Central Committee of the CPC. The merger of press groups originates from the direct decision and overall deployment of Shanghai municipal government management, and is aimed at carrying out the substantial merger of Shanghai's cultural industries by drawing on the experiences of other provinces in building media groups.

3. Major achievements of cultural system reform

Scientific and reasonable system design, coupled with powerful support and promotion, have enabled Shanghai to bring about successful cultural system reform, with a number of backbone cultural enterprises taking the lead. The quality literature and art produced in Shanghai are widely acknowledged and have won awards such as the 'Five 'One' Project' of spiritual civilization construction, the National Quality Stage Art Project, the 'Wenhua Award' and the 'Lotus Award'. Shanghai's local cultural enterprises have also featured in four successive lists of 'the top 30 cultural enterprises in China'. Thirteen cultural enterprises from Shanghai have listed Rmb ordinary shares (A-shares) or in the overseas market, and the securitization ratio of national assets in municipal-level propaganda systems reached 22.5% in 2012.[6] During the '11th five-year plan', Shanghai cultural industry achieved an average annual growth rate of 12%. Shanghai Zhangjiang National Innovation Demonstration Zone was listed in the first batch of national demonstration bases that integrate culture and technology, and a group of national-level industry bases jointly built by ministries and Shanghai city, such as the national digital publishing base, China (Shanghai) Network Audio-visual Industry Base and the National Green Creation Printing Demonstration Garden, play a leading role in the technological innovation of culture.

---

[6] Wu Bin. Increase of Impetus and Growth of Vitality: Accomplishment of the Phasal Task of Shanghai's Cultural System Reform [N], *Jiefang Daily*, November 13, 2012

> **Column 4-2 The 'Five 'One' Project'**
>
> The 'Five 'One' Project' appraisal activity, organized by the propaganda department of the CPC Central Committee, has been carried out annually since 1992, in which appraisal is based on the quality of cultural products made in the previous year in five categories: a good drama, good TV series (or a film), good book (only in social science), good theoretical article (only in social science), and good song. These products are organized, produced and recommended by provinces, autonomous regions and municipalities directly under the central government, along with some departments and ministries, and the general political department of the Chinese People's Liberation Army.

II. Supporting the development of cultural creation industries

In recent years, Shanghai has made a series of policies and measures to encourage the development of cultural creation industries. This has created a large number of new industrial styles that are composed of cultural elements, driven by creation, supported by technology and oriented by market, rapidly springing up and becoming new highlights in the development of Shanghai's cultural creation industries.

1. Optimizing the cultural creation industry layout

With proper layout and aggregation of characteristics, Shanghai has constructed a new spatial layout of cultural creative industries, which may be interpreted as 'one axis, two rivers, along the coast and multiple circles', so as to form an industry axis, industry belt and industry circle of the city's cultural creative industries. Shanghai implements a technology-as-impetus strategy to promote the integrated development of culture with finance, trade, information and tourism, focusing on the development of key creative projects to reinforce the core competitiveness of industries. The new industries, new types of operation and industry chains in cultural creative industries are fostered, with an emphasis placed on the media industry, art industry, industrial design, fashion, architectural design, network information, software, consulting services, advertising and exhibitions, and the entertainment industry. The construction of major cultural projects at both the national and local level has been accelerated, including the National Digital Publishing Base, National Animation and Game Industry Demonstration Area, National Music Industry Base, China (Shanghai) Network Audio-Visual Industry

Base, National Advertising Industry Demonstration Zone, National Green Creativity Printing Demonstration Zone, the pilot 'integration of three networks' project and NGB (Next Generation Broadcasting). The national-level cultural creative industry demonstration base has been constructed together with the renovation of old factory buildings, warehouses and wharfs. Then, Shanghai built a number of creative industry aggregation zones and creative industry service platforms, fostering well-known enterprises and brands in the creative industry and thereby forming a new growth point of cultural creative industries. Currently, Shanghai leads the country with as many as 114 cultural creative industry zones. In the zones, public service platforms keep growing in number, expanding from the original residential rent and property services to providing enterprise incubation, participating in enterprise development and offering financial services.

2. Fostering the cultural market main body

The opening of the cultural market is to be promoted, at the same time encouraging and leading the sound development of cultural enterprises with different types of ownership, and to form a development pattern that takes public ownership as the majority while various types of ownership develop together. State-owned or state-controlled cultural enterprises are supported and enhanced, and the modern enterprise system as well as corporate governance structure are perfected, so as to introduce strategic investors and promote the shareholding reform of state-owned cultural enterprises. Cultural creation enterprises are supported to be listed, and carry out acquisitions and reorganizations across regions, across industries and across ownership, fostering cultural enterprises with an output value worth Rmb10bn and backbone cultural enterprises with an output value of more than Rmb2bn. Social capital is allowed to be invested in certain cultural creative industries, and support is given to the establishment of strategic alliances between industry, university and research, with an emphasis on cultural technology enterprises and small and medium-sized cultural creativity enterprises that are 'specialized and new', innovative, and owning core technology and independent intellectual property rights. Shanghai attaches importance to fostering private non-enterprise and non-governmental cultural organizations, cultural creativity workshops and individual cultural business starters; consequently, a number of major cultural recreation projects have been initiated and accomplished in Shanghai. On August 16, 2009, China's largest amusement park, 'Shanghai Happy Valley', was opened. On April 8, 2011, Shanghai Disneyland holiday resort was officially launched, and in February 2012, 'Oriental DreamWorks', one of the largest Sino-foreign cooperation projects in cultural exchange, was signed between China and the US.

3. Striving to improve the environment of cultural creation industry

Shanghai vigorously promotes the platform construction of cultural property rights transaction, international cultural service trade, cultural creation industry sustained by finance, generic technology services of the cultural creation industry and cultural intermediary services. Five departments including the propaganda department of the Central Committee of the CPC established the national status of Shanghai Culture Exchange by issuing *On Implementing the Decision of the State Council to Reinforce the Administration of Cultural Assets and Equity Transaction and Artwork Transaction*. It also supported Shanghai Culture Assets and Equity Exchange to provide services for cultural enterprises and individuals across the country to transfer their assets of stock equity, obligatory rights, real rights and intellectual property rights, and in exploring the provision of value-added services. Cultural consumption is fostered and guided, and state-owned and private cultural agencies are encouraged to provide a certain number of sessions or tickets at lower prices. Measures are taken to provide citizens with more affordable public cultural products and services, such as books and journals, artistic performances and movies, so as to increase grassroots cultural consumption. The lever effect of state-owned cultural investment funds should be exerted, in order to encourage social capital investment in the cultural creation industry, innovate the development mode, channel, produce and serve the cultural creation industry sustained by finance, loan guarantee items suitable for the development of the cultural creation industry, and enhance financing services for small and medium-sized cultural creation enterprises. 'China Media Capital', the first cultural creation industry registered by the National Development and Reform Commission, has invested in major projects such as Star China and Oriental DreamWorks. Shanghai Creation (Design) Industry Investment Fund Alliance has been established, with Rmb28.2bn of gross capital under control. Shanghai researches and formulates a tax policy favorable to the development of the cultural creation industry, so that more of these enterprises are entitled to preferential policies such as reduced business tax and VAT rates. Shanghai also fosters and develops an 'IPO market' of cultural products and services, implementing a cultural brand strategy, reinforcing the protection of intellectual property rights, enhancing the comprehensive law enforcement of the cultural market, and guaranteeing the sound operation of the cultural market.

4. Accelerating the promotion of the international communication of cultural products and services

In recent years, Shanghai has made great efforts in areas such as accelerating the development of cultural creation service trade by relying on the construction of an international trade center, promoting the international communication of cultural creation products, and enlarging the trade of cultural creation products and services. In 2011, Shanghai international trade platform of cultural service was officially named by the Ministry of Culture as the 'national base for international cultural trade', and in the same year, gross imports and exports of Shanghai's cultural products and services reached US$16.62bn, up 10.9% year on year, realizing a trade surplus of US$3.45bn. In the fields of press and publications, radio, film and television, culture and art, and digital entertainment, some cultural creative enterprises have qualified for 'going global'. Shanghai Century Publishing House published *The China Wave* in 2011, with a print run of more than 600,000 copies, and its traditional Chinese character version has been published in Hong Kong, with an English translation already initiated. The multimedia theatrical event, ERA – Intersection of Times, has put on a show every day to earn export revenues. Between 2005 and 2011 the show was performed 2,479 times, grossing Rmb260m at the box office, 70% of which was foreign exchange earnings since 70% of the 2.49m audience were foreigners. BesTV promotes the export of internet protocol television (IPTV) technology to countries such as France and Indonesia. On September 29, 2013, as China (Shanghai) Pilot Free Trade Zone officially started operations, the Ministry of Culture issued *Notice on the Implementation of the Cultural Market Administration Policies in China (Shanghai) Pilot Free Trade Zone*, giving explanations about the 'introduction' of cultural products and services. The Notice proposed that foreign-run entertainment venues are allowed to be established in the pilot zone; foreign performance broker agencies can now invest as wholly foreign-owned entities, rather than as joint ventures, and are permitted to provide services to Shanghai citizens; game and recreation facilities that have passed the examination of the competent cultural department are entitled to make domestic sales. All the policies contribute to the prosperity of Shanghai's culture and the reinforcement of its creative vitality.

III. Vigorously developing public cultural service

Shanghai municipal party committee and municipal government repeatedly stress that public cultural service must stick to the principles of common good, fundamentality, equality and convenience, with the government playing a dominant role and the grassroots being the focus, so as to build a public cultural service system covering urban and rural areas and benefiting everyone. With public finance being the support, and the guarantee of basic needs being the standard, the facility layout is still to be perfected. Content supply is guaranteed so as to innovate the system mechanism, enhance the service benefit, and improve the quality of citizens' cultural lives. After years of effort, Shanghai tops the country in terms of the construction of a public cultural service system.

Picture 4-1 China Art Palace (Photographed by reporter, Ren Long, of Xinhua News Agency)

1. Balanced development of public cultural facilities

In light of urban and rural development integration, Shanghai has planned and constructed public cultural facilities in a balanced way, integrated functions and convenient services, and has improved the three-level public cultural service system composed of key cultural facilities at municipal level, cultural activity centers at district level and cultural activity centers at community level. A number of major public cultural facilities have been established, with the focus laid upon the construction and reconstruction of municipal-level facilities such as China Art Palace, Power Station of Art, World Expo Museum, Shanghai Children's Art Theatre, Shanghai History Museum and Hongqiao International Dance Center; the World Expo Puxi Garden has been also been planned. The construction of community cultural activity centers across the city has been further improved in terms of layout, and by the end of 2012, the following facilities had been built: 32 art galleries; 238 public libraries; 120 museums, memorial halls and exhibition halls; 26 cultural centers at district level, 203 community cultural activity centers, and 5,245 village (neighborhood) comprehensive cultural activity rooms; 19 workers' cultural palaces (clubs); 36 youth activity centers, children's palaces, children's science stations and activity campsites; and more than 100 public cultural activity squares that can accommodate 200-1,500 people. Public cultural facilities across the whole city cover 3m square meters, and the target of a public cultural service being within a 15- minute radius was put forward in the '11th five-year plan' has been realized.

2. Further improving the efficiency of the public cultural service system

The first aspect is the in-depth development of cultural venues open to the public and free of charge. In 2012, municipal-level libraries, cultural centers, community cultural activity centers, as well as state-run art galleries at municipal and district level, opened to the public free of charge, with some elementary services also free of charge. Out of the 120 museums, memorial halls and exhibition halls, more than 80 are open to the public free of charge. The second is the digital public cultural service network in full swing. Conspicuous achievements have been made in constructing next-generation radio and television. The municipal government promotes the approval of some major projects, such as the gradual digitization of rural cable television networks. For example, by 2012 the cooperative project of the State Administration of Radio, Film and Television and the municipal city achieved the integral transition of rural cable television digitalization for 1m households, and NGB construction for 1m households in both urban and rural areas. The demonstration network has gradually expanded to the districts of Minhang, Pudong, Songjiang, Baoshan, Qingpu and Jiading, thereby encompassing 4m NGB households across the whole city. Shanghai has also vigorously set up an information-issuing platform of public cultural services, and in 2012, it issued a public cultural service information map, and a 'central supervisory information system of community cultural activity centers' was also put online. The third aspect is the constant coverage expansion of public cultural services. In 2012, more than 300 subsidized performances were shown in 14 theaters, with a full range of performances, and the new performance brands were welcomed by the audience. Shanghai is also enhancing the opening of various public cultural facilities to migrant workers, improving the migrant worker-oriented serving capabilities of communities, and thus the entitlement to public cultural service of vulnerable and marginalized groups. Various public cultural facilities in the city have created barrier-free access, and there are children's reading rooms in most libraries, and more than 200 'sunshine homes' have been established for the 70,000 mentally disabled in the city.

3. Constant innovative developments in public cultural activities

The variety of mass culture brand activities in Shanghai is becoming more influential, highlighting the cultural brand effect that equates Shanghai as an international cultural metropolis. China Shanghai International Arts Festival is designed to fully explore urban cultural connotations, inherit the splendid national culture, with importance attached to the design and development of new fields and new projects. During the festival, multilayered national and international cultural exchange events are performed to a large audience, thus realizing its ambition to be a 'festival of the masses'. 'Shanghai Spring' mass cultural activities are designed to popularize communication, lead and encourage participation, promote and support original creation, and find and foster talent. As a result, a large number of Shanghai citizens and tourists can appreciate the splendor and charm of the music festival through various channels. In addition, Shanghai Book Fair and Shanghai International Literature Week have an ever-growing influence, and many grassroots mass cultural brand activities keep springing up, such as 'Literary Shanghai introduced to communities', 'high art introduced to campuses', 'weekly performance', 'joy journey to the countryside', 'joy journey to construction sites', 'citizen art exhibitions' and 'grand stage of the masses'. Therefore, a cultural scene has been formed, where there are joint performances every season, performances every month and activities every day. Shanghai also vigorously promotes the construction of government body culture, enterprise culture, trade culture, campus culture, construction site culture, community culture, countryside culture, and family culture, thus consolidating the cultural foundation of the grassroots.

4. The ever-progressing system mechanism of public cultural services

Shanghai stimulates social forces to participate in the construction of a public cultural service system. The first is to guide social forces to participate in public cultural services with policies, and encourage social forces to get involved in initiating cultural undertakings for the public such as museums, libraries and art galleries. The second is the reinforcement of collaboration between the government and enterprises. The third is the popularization of the specialized management mode for public cultural socialization, and a group of cultural institutions and organizations qualified for socialization and specialization are fostered and developed. The fourth is the establishment of the democratic management mechanism in community cultural activity centers. Shanghai strives to inherit and protect cultural relics and improve the protection and inheritance mechanism of its intangible cultural heritage. The city has also accelerated the Shanghai Yuan Dynasty Water Gate Museum and Songze Museum of Ancient Ruins projects, and initiated the editing of *The Illustrated Directory Dictionary of Shanghai's Intangible Cultural Heritage* (Volume 2) and the electronic map plotting of Shanghai Intangible Cultural Heritage, thus improving the protection, inheritance, administration and employment of its historical and cultural heritage. On April 1, 2013 the *Regulations of Shanghai Community Public Cultural Services* were officially implemented. They were the first local regulations in the country aimed at community public cultural services, and therefore played a significant role in improving community public cultural services, guaranteeing the basic cultural rights of the masses, and propelling the construction of Shanghai's public cultural service system.

IV. Prospering and developing urban tourism

Urban tourism, based on hub-like transportation facilities and the developed tourism accommodation that exists in big cities, includes activities such as sightseeing, shopping, business, exhibitions, science and education, leisure and festivals, and it is an important carrier of a city's image. Shanghai's urban tourism is developing from sightseeing to in-depth tours and experience tourism, and in this respect, culture plays a vital role.

1. Formulating and implementing the development strategy of urban tourism

In 1997, Shanghai officially put forward the concept of 'urban tourism', defining the orientation of Shanghai tourism as urban tourism. The development is targeted at fully taking advantage of humanistic resources and the resources of the city as an economic center, and at fully exerting the functions of new scenes in the city and its comprehensive functions, so as to develop tourist products that integrate urban scenes, urban culture and urban business. At a Shanghai tourism working conference in 2001, it was clearly put forward that the city should foster a world-class tourism brand, develop urban tourism and build an international touring metropolis. The tour slogan of Shanghai is 'Seven Wonders of The World, Seven Days in Shanghai', and the logo is a colorful one that highlights the city flower, *Magnolia denudata*. In April 2010, in support of Shanghai World Expo, the National Tourism Administration and Shanghai municipal government jointly issued the logo and slogan 'Shanghai China – More Discovery, More Experience'.

In recent years, Shanghai urban tourism has been aimed at satisfying the cultural needs of tourists to take leisure holidays, and thus health-oriented leisure tourism and eco-tourism have rapidly developed, with Nanhui Peach Flower Festival, Changxing Orange Festival and Fengxian Rape Flower Festival being among the highlights. When it comes to a tourist destination, Shanghai citizens will give top priority to destinations that are close to nature, full of delight in the wild, quiet and peaceful, and with clean air. The distinctive urban tourism aimed at foreign and domestic tourists, such as exhibition tourism, business tourism, tourism aimed at different races and industrial and agricultural tourism, have developed even more rapidly. In 2012, the number of domestic tourists totaled 250.9m person-visits, while that of international tourists reached 8.004m person-visits, which not only brought considerable tourism revenues for Shanghai, but also stimulated employment and gave rise to market prosperity.

Figure 4-2 The opening of Nanhui peach flower festival (Photographed by reporter Liu Ying, Xinhua News Agency)

2. Accelerating the construction of key tourist projects

To build more and better urban tourist destinations, Shanghai has initiated a large batch of key tourist projects that have reinforced its attraction as an urban tourism destination. The intensive development of Shanghai Sheshan National Tourist and Holiday Resort, Fengxian Gulf Tourist Resort, Jinshan City Beach, the area along Dianshan Lake and Chongming Island tourism has motivated the rapid development of rural tourism. The comprehensive service functions of some distinctive tourist streets have been improved, such as the Bund, Nanjing Road, Huaihai Road and Hengshan Road, which may fully represent the humanistic spirit and historical context of Shanghai. The forming of modern service industry agglomeration areas, such as Huangpu river-Suzhou creek agglomeration belt, the loop around People's Square, Shanghai New World, Nanjing Road West, Huaihai Road, the north Bund, Changfeng area and Xujiahui, has contributed to the establishment of tourism as a distinctive and leading sector. Some projects under construction have added more charm and attraction to Shanghai urban tourism, such as Disneyland Theme Park and its supporting facilities, Jinhai Lake in Nanqiao New Town, the Wu and Yue Boundary River culture tourist area in the ancient town of Jinshan Fengjing, and the comprehensive tourist project in the center of Xujiahui. Besides attracting tourist projects, the 'hub' program – Shanghai Tourist Distributing Center, aimed at satisfying the demands of high-quality tours – was also moved to its new home in April 2012, and its multiple functions, including consultancy, ticket services, handling tourist complaints and tourist safety administration, have made contributions to the building of Shanghai as a world-famous tourist city.

3. Subdividing and solidifying the tourist commodity categories

Shanghai urban tourism was initiated in 1997, and over the next 15 years, it was subdivided and solidified into several categories, including business and exhibitions, cruises and yachts, specific theme experience and festival celebrations, shopping and gourmet, urban leisure, rural weekend holidays and museum culture. Of these categories, business exhibition tourism is a distinctive element in Shanghai urban tourism, for business exhibitions in Shanghai are numerous, large in scale and high in quality, which may fully represent the feature of Shanghai city as an international economic center. The International Congress and Convention Association revealed that Shanghai held 72 international association conferences in 2012, and ranked 35th in the world out of all cities to hold such events. In addition, Shanghai also initiated an 'urban golden circle' sightseeing bus tour comprising many routes. On the sightseeing bus, commentary in eight languages is provided, with a day pass ticket being applicable at all stops and routes that take in well-known scenic spots and shopping malls. These beautiful open double-decker buses pass through scenic streets and other beauty spots.

4. Serving the World Expo and improving the tourist environment

While Shanghai made preparations for the 2010 World Expo and then during the event itself, which was centered on the theme of 'Better city, better life' and was run on the basis of 'Serving the World Expo and serving tourists', Shanghai managed to combine the right equipment and tourist facilities through coordination across departments, establishing a link between the city and districts, and the participation of society, with the construction of a World Expo tourist public service system being the support, and the improvement of tourist comprehensive service levels being the focus. In addition, Shanghai provided standardized, internationalized, modernized and humanized World Expo touring services; developed rich, colorful and attractive World Expo tourism products; and fostered a safe, convenient and comfortable touring environment, so as to provide tourists with a splendid 'Experiencing the World Expo tour' with 'More discovery, more experience', and an in-depth Shanghai tour as well. All these successfully interpreted the World Expo theme of 'Better city, better life', representing the beautiful scenery and urban charm of Shanghai, and creating an enthusiastic and friendly urban atmosphere that provided visitor support, facility support, service support, profit support and sustainability support for the success, splendor and legacy of the World Expo. During the World Expo, tourist agencies organized more than 8,000 tour buses, more than 20,000 World Expo guides and the World Expo park received 73.08m person-visits, including 668,000 tour groups, 20.877m person-visits by groups, accounting for 28.57% of the total number of visitors to the park.

Prior to the opening of the World Expo, to provide the tourists with more convenient services, Shanghai co-operated with Jiangsu and Zhejiang to issue and implement *Specifications of Road Traffic Signs in Tourist Scenic Areas*. These coffee-colored traffic sign specifications were designed for self-drive travelers and tour buses, and not only conformed with developed European and American countries in terms of color design, showing internationally compatible features, but were also scientifically located in a way that was consistent with the jointly enforced specifications, which showed scientificity, uniformity and aesthetic beauty. Through the specifications, Shanghai realized the target of integrating road traffic signs in the Yangtze River Delta's scenic areas.

5. Constantly improving the people's livelihood function of tourism

The construction of a public information service network as the support has constantly enhanced the people's livelihood function of Shanghai's tourism consultancy system. Such a system is composed of three longitudinal information network levels and five horizontal informational network items, with the former comprising: Shanghai tourist hotline 962020, 45 tourist consultancy service centers and more than 400 tourist touch-screens, and the latter comprising: the government affairs website of Shanghai tourism, Shanghai tour website, Shanghai tour human resource website, Shanghai tour distribution website and Shanghai tour exhibition website. Currently, 45 tourist consultancy service centers have been established in crowded sites such as airports, ports, railway stations, major commercial blocks and scenic spots and they have received as many as 2.3m tourist visits, and have distributed more than 10m tour maps and scenic spot booklets.

> **Column 4-3 Ninety-nine reasons for loving Shanghai**
>
> The '99 reasons to love Shanghai' initiative by Shanghai Tourism Administration and other agencies was the result of a survey of netizens asked to post their reasons for enjoying the city. On January 6, 2013, through the official microblog 'Happy Tour in Shanghai', Shanghai Tourism Administration published 99 reasons for loving Shanghai, which were selected out of the 600,000 reasons supplied by net friends. This activity drew the interest of nearly 36m net friends.
>
> "Here in Shanghai, I can hardly tell why I love Shanghai," said one net friend. "But when I leave for another city, I suddenly realize there are an inexhaustible number of reasons for loving Shanghai…
>
> "Shanghainese are reasonable; Shanghainese are clear-minded; Shanghainese have a sharp tongue but a warm heart; Shanghainese are fashionable, and Shanghai is a city of beautiful women and handsome men."

At the end of March 2011, Shanghai Tourism Administration opened the official microblog 'Happy Tour in Shanghai', with a focus on food, accommodation, transportation, touring, shopping and recreation. The microblog released the latest tourist information to the public, and addressed questions and problems of tourists by means of a Q&A, which won the positive appraisal of tourists. In the two years since it was online, the microblog released more than 10,000 tourist information messages, attracting more than 690,000 Sina microblog fans.

In 2012, Shanghai municipal government listed the activity of 'tourism information conveyed to communities' as a practical project. A first batch of 100 community cultural activity centers were chosen to establish tourism information stations, so as to expand tourism information services to communities. In addition, 'e-tour' touch-screen systems were established in these community cultural activity centers as well as Shanghai's star-rated hotels, with the information in Chinese, English and Japanese, and covering the six tourist themes of 'catering, accommodation, transportation, sightseeing, shopping and recreation'. Such systems were of great help to foreign and domestic tourists. The Shanghai tourist hotlines '12301' and '962020' are 'call centers' that provide 24-hour Chinese and English telephone consultation services, which is rarely found in other Chinese cities. A 'mobile phone guide' is being developed in line with the construction of Shanghai smart city, and such services include navigation, tour guides and GPS location through smart phones, which can help tourists answer questions such as 'Where am I?', 'Where do I go?' and 'How do I get there?'

6. Maintaining the integrated development of tourism

With the transformation of tourism upgrades, integration has become a key task in the future development of tourism. After more than 10 years of rapid development, the orientation of Shanghai's urban tourism is being transformed from quantity to quality. Through industrial and regional integration, Shanghai has achieved good economic profits and social benefits in urban tourism, with improvements in width, depth and range.

In terms of industrial integration, Shanghai reinforces collaboration with departments such as industry, agriculture, propaganda, development and reform, the establishment of diplomatic relations, culture, finance, sports, education, science and technology, medicine and meteorology, with priority given to the development of exhibition tourism, cultural tourism, sports tourism, health care tourism, gourmet tourism and cruise tourism, thus realizing the diversification of tourist resources and the facilitation of tourist services. For instance, a 'night culture' industry has injected new vigor into urban tourism capacity and output value by highlighting the great charm of old Shanghai songs such as *Night Shanghai and Night Willow Herb*. In the second half of 2012, Shanghai Tourism Administration and the cultural and broadcasting departments of Shanghai jointly signed *The Three-year Action Plan of Shanghai Cultural Tourism Development*, according to which, prior to 2015, Shanghai was built as an international urban cultural tourist destination, which inherited Shanghai's regional culture, integrated its folk customs, led the civilization mode, and assembled festivals and competitions. Such a plan provided cultural support for Shanghai in building a world-famous tourist city, and consolidated the industrial base for the building of an international cultural metropolis.

In terms of regional integration, remarkable achievements have also been made in recent years, in terms of the establishment of a top-level coordination mechanism of the Yangtze River Delta integration development, and by the mutual support of tourist products across provinces and a series of product innovations. In 2011, the tourism authorities in Jiangsu province, Zhejiang province and Shanghai city jointly formulated the *Three-year Action Plan of Researching, Developing and Popularizing the 'Theme+Experience' Series of Tourist Products in Yangtze River Delta City Groups*, vigorously promoting R&D and popularizing the 'Theme+Experience' series of tourist products in Yangtze River Delta city groups, demonstrating with multiple options and multiple layers Yangtze River Delta world-class city groups such as the rich living elements, the beautiful natural environment, the deep cultural connotations, and a tourist environment of fairness and integrity, and providing a standardized, normalized and qualified service. The integrated development of regional tourism enables the integrated tourism of the Yangtze River Delta to step into a new phase of 'urban commonality', in which tourism resources are integrated; tourist products are jointly researched and developed; the tourist market is jointly promoted; and tourism achievements are shared. Such integrated development also enables Shanghai urban tourism to acquire new hinterland support and growth potential. In the Yangtze River Delta region, tourists are particularly attracted to festivals, and therefore, since 2012, just for their convenience, Shanghai Tourism Administration has made joint efforts with the Meteorological Bureau to initiate a Yangtze River Delta tourist city weather forecast and an index of geographical data, which has been favorably received by the citizen tourists.

Chapter 4

In recent years, tourism has become a key industry in Shanghai's tertiary sector as well as a dynamic industry in the modern service industry. Urban tourism has become a noted brand of Shanghai tourism and an established industry of the city. Currently, Shanghai urban tourism is entering a transition phase, as it passes from the initial phase to the mature phase. The major task of this phase is to integrate the product system, enlarge the industrial scale, optimize the industrial structure, and upgrade the industrial energy level, which may lay solid foundations for tourism to become a distinctive industry in Shanghai's economic structure and to become a key carrier of Shanghai's urban image.

Chapter 5

The Protection and Renovation of Shanghai's Ecological Environment

Shanghai is a city with a dense population and scarce natural resources, and also one with a high degree of industrialization and limited environmental capacity. The urban ecosystem is comparatively fragile, and the harmony between economic development and the ecological environment is of paramount significance to the city. Therefore, environmental protection is one of the key elements of Shanghai's development. In recent years, Shanghai has constantly reinforced the protection of the ecological environment, and has formed an initial set of efficient policy systems and working mechanisms, which has been sufficient to guarantee the sustainable development of Shanghai's economy and society.

I. The rolling implementation of environmental protection and three-year action plans

Ecological environment protection in Shanghai is mainly realized by *Shanghai's Five-year Plan of Environmental Protection and Ecological Construction* and *Shanghai's Three-year Action Plan of Environmental Protection and Construction*.

1. Shanghai's five-year plan of environmental protection and ecological construction

Shanghai's Five-year Plan of Environmental Protection and Ecological Construction is a specialized plan of *The Five-year Plan of Shanghai's National Economy and Social Development*, and on the basis of the allotted time of five years, the 11th five-year plan of environmental protection between 2005 and 2010 has been fulfilled, with the 12th five-year plan between 2011 and 2015 currently under way. The plan covers areas such as water environment protection, air environment protection, multipurpose use and disposal of solid waste, industrial pollution protection, agriculture and rural environment protection, and ecological environment construction. In terms of expenditure on environment protection, Shanghai spends more than 3% of its GDP on environmental protection each year. During the 11th five-year plan, Shanghai environmental protection spending amounted to Rmb206.7bn.

Shanghai's biggest project in terms of environmental protection is the comprehensive treatment of Suzhou Creek, also known as the Wusong river, which is one of the most important rivers in Shanghai. The direct discharge of untreated industrial and domestic wastewater, as well as the effect of shipping and port operations, caused severe pollution of Suzhou Creek. Up to the 1970s, it had become a serious environment problem affecting people's lives. In the 1980s, Shanghai initiated treatment of the creek, and in 1996, the municipal government established the Leading Group of Suzhou Creek Treatment, starting the systematic treatment of Suzhou Creek.

The first-stage project of Suzhou Creek treatment lasted from 1998 to 2002, with a total investment of Rmb7bn. It was aimed at improving water quality, the land environment and adjacent river system, so that the black and fetid main stream of the creek and at the junction of Suzhou river and Huangpu river could be eliminated. The messy and dirty environment along both banks of the river was addressed, and 10 projects categorized into three types were constructed for the purpose of building green belts along the river. In addition, a large quantity of research was carried out. As a result, by 2000, the black and fetid main stream of Suzhou Creek had almost been eliminated, and the leading indicators of water quality kept improving year after year.

The second-stage project of Suzhou Creek treatment was carried out between 2003 and 2005 with a total investment of Rmb4bn, for the purpose of improving the water quality, land environment and green space developments. Eight projects were involved in this stage, in areas such as sewage interception and treatment, green space developments along both banks and the relocation of wharves to improve environmental sanitation.

The third stage project of Suzhou Creek treatment was carried out between 2006 and 2008 with a total investment of Rmb3.14bn. The core task was water quality, aimed at treating the river once and for all, and great importance was attached to sewage interception and treatment. Sediment dredging was carried out, and flood control walls and a greener landscape along both sides were built. In total, four projects were implemented that were aimed at improving water quality and restoring the water ecosystem.

After these three project stages, the treatment of Suzhou Creek has been successful, with the black color and fetid smell eliminated, and the water quality stable. Fish have returned, and water quality in the tributaries has improved; the waterway has been cleaned and the city's overall appearance has been changed for the better. The implementation of these projects has changed the overall appearance of Suzhou Creek, and the quality of life for residents has been improved, which has resulted in a substantial appreciation of land values along both sides of the waterway and has yielded huge profit for real estate companies. The area surrounding Suzhou Creek has become one of most desirable leisure areas in Shanghai, and tourists from all over the world have been attracted to the clean water and green banks, and to the elegant architectural landscapes along the two banks. As a result, the tourist economy has boomed.

2. Shanghai's three-year environmental protection and construction action plan

Shanghai's Three-year Action Plan of Environmental Protection and Construction is a concrete plan of *Shanghai's Five-year Plan Environmental Protection and Ecological Construction* (the planned tasks are divided and carried out in every single year), and three years is the allotted time, with the plan implemented in a rolling fashion.

Shanghai's Three-year Action Plan of Environmental Protection and Construction, which was initiated in 2000, was designed to address the city's environmental problems and improve the environment quality. Up to 2012, Shanghai had implemented four rounds of three-year action plans of environmental protection, solving in different stages the environmental problems against the backdrop of rapid industrialization and urbanization. As a result, the environment infrastructure system and ecological pattern have been basically formed, and treatment in some key areas has been effective, with the environment administration system and urban environment quality constantly improved. In the fourth round of the three-year action plan of environmental protection, Shanghai exceeded the pollution reduction target of the '11th five-year plan', with the total emissions of chemical oxygen demand and sulfur dioxide being 27.7% and 30.2% respectively, ranking among the top performers in the country. A 'good' ambient air quality has been achieved more than 90% of the time for three consecutive years, and the concentration of pollutants such as sulfur dioxide, nitrogen dioxide and inhalable particles has been reduced by 41%, 9% and 10%, respectively, compared with 2008. In addition, the environmental quality of the main body of water has remained stable.

II. Implementing domain-oriented energy conservation and emission reduction

With the development of the economy and the improvement in people's living conditions, the total energy consumed in Shanghai has kept on increasing. In 2012, the total energy consumed in Shanghai was 113.6215m tons of standard coal, with a per capita energy consumption of 4.84 tons of standard coal. To decrease energy consumption and enhance environmental protection, Shanghai has taken energy conservation and emission reduction measures to lower unit energy consumption, improve energy efficiency and reduce the emission of pollutants.

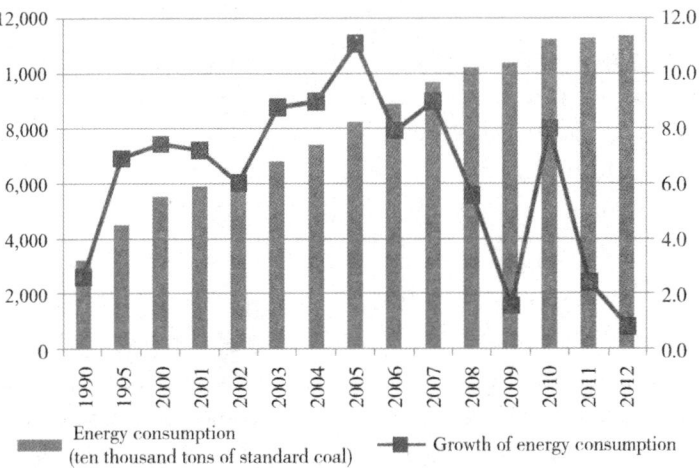

Figure 5-1 Energy consumption growth in Shanghai 1990-2012 (ten thousand tons of standard coal)

In terms of energy consumption and pollution, Shanghai has emphasized energy conservation and emission reduction in the three biggest and most concentrated areas of industry, construction and transportation.

1. Energy conservation and emission reduction in the industrial sector

The industrial sector in Shanghai is a focus of energy conservation and emission reduction. On the one hand, by means of industrial restructuring, Shanghai promotes the acceleration of the upgrading of high-energy-consumption and high-pollution industries, and accelerates the elimination of outdated

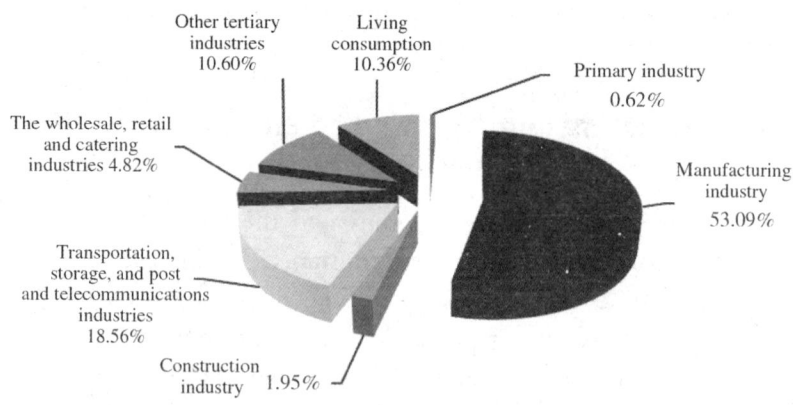

Figure 5-2 The structure of energy consumption in Shanghai, 2012

production capacity, phasing out cement factories and small-scale smelters along with other industries using outdated techniques. On the other hand, technology upgrading is vigorously promoted to realize energy conservation and emission reduction. For instance, the technological upgrading of industrial boilers has helped to realize the target of saving coal, using technologies such as efficient combustion technology, steam heat accumulator technology, draught fan and pump frequency conversion technology, intelligent control technology and heat supply network optimization management technology.

Power plants are the main energy supplier in the city, and the largest consumer of coal. More than 90% of installed power-generating capacity in Shanghai is in the form of coal-fired units. Shanghai has organized technological research on the development of supercritical coal-fired power generation, and designed supercritical coal-fired power generator sets suitable for China's specific types of coal. As a result, energy consumption has been lowered and generating efficiency improved, with coal-fired units reducing coal consumption by as much as 20%.

For the purpose of energy conservation, the clean utilization of coal has also contributed to emissions reduction. For instance, Shanghai Waigaoqiao Power Generating Company has installed four sets of 300,000 kw coal-fired units, with an installed gross capacity of 1.2m kw, becoming one of the most important electricity generation bases in Shanghai. Through the application of low nitrogen oxide combustion technology, the emission of oxynitrides has fallen 40%, and the company was the first to establish a flue gas desulfurization power plant in Shanghai. In 2007, the amount of desulfurization achieved by Waigaoqiao Power Generating Company accounted for 46% of Shanghai's total amount.

2. Energy conservation in construction

Shanghai has rapidly developed residential and public architecture, and the energy consumption element of architecture has also grown. Energy conservation and consumption reduction in architecture is concerned with two main issues: one is the inadequate thermal insulation and airtightness of buildings, and the other is the large energy consumption of air conditioners and other household appliances. Therefore, Shanghai has established a technological system of energy-saving architecture. Since 2001, a series of research projects have been carried out, and in 2004, the design standards for energy-saving architecture was worked out. New houses must adhere to such standards; otherwise, construction will not be approved. Compared with standards in the 1980s, the energy conservation of new houses can reach 50%, in terms of walls, windows and doors, air conditioners and lighting. In Songjiang and Jiading districts, energy-saving and 'zero' consumption detached houses and energy-saving demonstration apartments of 600,000 square meters have been popularized.

Compared with residential architecture, public architecture is on a bigger scale and is therefore a larger consumer of energy. On the basis of the optimal integration of technology, Shanghai has applied energy-saving transformation technology to many public buildings and established large-scale, real-time monitoring platforms that measure the energy consumption of public buildings. For example, Shanghai Pudong International Airport employs special glass coatings, natural ventilation, water storage and rainwater reuse, thereby saving 130m kilowatt hours of electricity over the course of a year, equivalent to 54.9% of what it used to consume.

3. Energy conservation and emission reduction in transportation

Car ownership in Shanghai has increased dramatically in recent years, resulting in problems such as high fuel consumption and exhaust emissions. In response, Shanghai has prioritized the development of public transportation. Great efforts have been made to construct the subway system, and by adopting the 'subway-bus' connection mode, citizens are encouraged to use public transport more and private cars less. Shanghai has also sought to develop new alternative energy, improve the fuel economy of motor vehicles and develop new energy automobiles. In order to tackle the deficiencies of the traditional trolley bus, Shanghai has supported the R&D of a super-capacitor bus; bus line 11 running on the China loop line starting and ending at the City God Temple is the first super-capacitor bus line in the world, contains features such as zero emissions, energy conservation, low noise and flexible operation. Two years of test runs comprising 800,00km testified the zero emissions, and an electricity consumption of only 100 kilowatt hours every 100km, with energy recuperation exceeding 40%. At the 2010 World Expo, Shanghai employed similar 'green transport' vehicles.

During the '11th five-year plan', Shanghai accomplished the target of a 20% decrease in energy consumption for every Rmb10,000 GDP by 2010, as required by the country. Therefore, Shanghai formulated the '10 measures of energy conservation and emission reduction' through which the target of a 20% decrease was accomplished, with the fall in sulfur dioxide and chemical oxygen demand being 30.2% and 27.71%, respectively, ranking second best and best performance in the country.

Column 5-1 Shanghai's '10 measures of energy conservation and emission reduction'

(1) Strictly controlling high energy consumption and high pollution industries. Through the strict practice of industry policy, strict control of newly built projects and strict control over total energy consumption, high energy consumption and high pollution industries can be urged to realize structural adjustment and upgrading.

(2) Accelerating the phasing out of outdated production capacity, such as the cement and smelting industries, and backward techniques.

(3) Promoting 'the development of large projects while suppressing small ones' in the electric power industry. Small thermal units have been closed, as planned, and new electric power projects are promoted.

(4) Strengthening the energy-saving management of key energy-consuming units. The focus of supervision and management is laid on the 'big families' in energy consumption, so that they could reach the standard.

(5) Reinforcing energy-saving management in key fields. The focus should be placed on architecture energy conservation and transportation conservation, and the development and utilization of renewable resources should be encouraged.

(6) Promoting the technological advance of energy conservation and emission reduction. The R&D and industrialization of key technologies of new forms of energy are encouraged to accelerate the construction of energy-saving

technology. The key projects of energy conservation and emission reduction are implemented to propel the extensive application of energy-saving technology.

(7) Fully playing the role of price leverage. Through implementing national policies such as differential electricity prices, energy conservation, environmental protection and new resource utilization can be promoted.

(8) Increasing expenditure on energy conservation and emission reduction. An input mechanism should be established, according to which the government leads, enterprises play the main part and the whole of society participates, so that social capital could be led to invest in energy conservation and emission reduction projects.

(9) Reinforcing the construction of pollution-reduction projects. The construction of sewage infrastructure and electric power plant desulfurization projects should be propelled.

(10) Enhancing the supervision of pollution reduction. In addition to reinforcing supervisory control over the total amount of pollutant discharge, pollution-reduction checks should also be strengthened, and reduction statistics in the city and all districts and counties, and all institutions, should be released regularly.

III. Vigorously promoting the planning and building of an ecological green land system

A green land system is the only living infrastructure in the city, and it is an important foundation for the sustainable development of an urban society and economy. Getting the city closer to nature and integrated into nature is a main theme of the city's future afforestation development. Shanghai attaches great importance to the urban ecological green land system, and after years of planning and building, the urban green land area and urban afforestation coverage has increased, which has provided an agreeable ecological environment for citizens. The building of an ecological green land system in Shanghai has been mainly implemented by means of the overall city plan, the specific planning of ecological green land and the five-year plan.

1. The Urban Master Plan of Shanghai City (1999-2020) and The Urban Green Land System Planning of Shanghai City (2002-2020)

The Urban Master Plan of Shanghai City (1999-2020) proposes that the key point is the construction of a 'ring, wedge, porch and garden' in the central city, and large areas of artificial forest in the suburban areas, for the purpose of improving the urban ecological environment. Up to 2020, the per capita public green land index will be above 10 square meters, and the per capita green land index will be above 20 square meters, with an afforestation coverage ratio exceeding 35%. In the central city, every district is required to develop public green land area of at least four hectares, and every sub-district a green land area of one hectare, and every suburban county or town a public green land area of three hectares. It is also required that a greenbelt should be built along rivers and roads, and that large-scale forest parks and green land wedges should be built. In the city, there are designated urban ecology sensitive areas and urban construction sensitive areas, so as to protect the urban landscape, and protect birds in Chongming Dongtan, baby Chinese sturgeon in the Yangtze estuary and natural protection areas such as the Jiuduansha Wetland.

The Urban Green Land System Planning of Shanghai City (2002-2020) is the detailed plan of *The Urban Master Plan of Shanghai City (1999-2020)*, according to which, in the light of the optimal afforestation ecological effect and its relation with the frequency of the prevailing wind direction, and in combination with agricultural restructuring, Shanghai plans to construct its urban area with all levels of public green land being the focus, and its suburban areas with large-scale ecological forest being the main body, and then the areas along the 'river, lake, sea, road, island and city' with a greenbelt being the network and connection. In this way, the great circulation of urban afforestation may come into being, in which the 'main body' may interact with the 'focus' through the 'network', and the overall layout of the urban afforestation is thus 'ring, wedge, patch, garden and forest', with the city being in the forest and the people in the green, which in turn lays foundation for Shanghai in forest, or green Shanghai.

The Urban Master Plan of Shanghai City (1999-2020) and *The Urban Green Land System Planning of Shanghai City (2002-2020)* constitute the basic frame for the construction of ecological green land in Shanghai.

2. Shanghai's five-year plan ecological green land construction

Shanghai formulates its 'five-year plan of city afforestation' every five years, which is the specifically designed plan of 'Shanghai's Five-year Plan of National Economy and Social Development'.

In the period of the accomplished *'11th Five-year Plan' of Shanghai City Afforestation (2005-2010)*, Shanghai realized a breakthrough development in ecological green land construction. The newly built green land area in Shanghai reached 6,600 hectares, and the afforestation coverage ratio increased from 37% in 2005 to 38.15% in 2010, and per capita public green space increased from 11.01 square meters to 13 square meters over the same period, with the forest coverage reaching 12.58%.

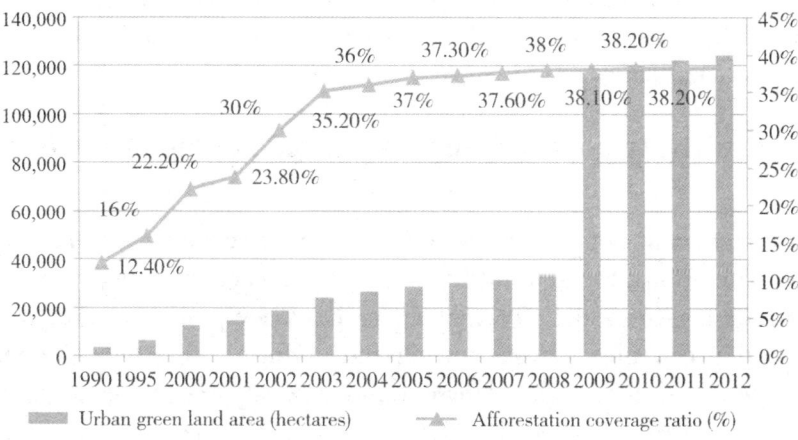

Figure 5-3 Shanghai green land construction between 1990 and 2012

In addition, it was put forward in the *12th Five-year Plan of Shanghai's National Economy and Social Development* that a green ecological homeland agreeable for living should be built, and a basic ecological network that is multilayered, connective and multi-functional should be established. By 2015, forest coverage reached 15%, with the afforestation coverage ratio standing at 38.5%. To reach this goal, some further plans were made in the *12th Five-year Plan of Shanghai's City Afforestation*. The downtown area still forms the 'ring, wedge, patch and garden' as the main body, and the surrounding area is reinforced by an urban greenbelt and ecological space, and the whole urban area is based on an ecological corridor, ecological conservation and natural wetland, thus forming the start of a basic ecological network space system frame with an 'annular radial pattern'. Emphasis is placed on the implementation of 'two rings, three belts, four patches, six wedges, 10 corridors and multiple gardens'. The two rings are the two greenbelts along the outer ring road and suburban ring road, with different widths. The three belts refer to the three coastal backbone forest belts along the north of Chongming, the coast of Pudong and the coastline of Hangzhou Bay. The four patches are the anti-pollution isolating greenbelts around the large-scale industrial areas and the garbage disposal bases in the petrochemical areas, Wujing chemical area, Shanghai chemical industry zone and Baoshan Baosteel. The five areas are the Chongming Dongtan

Bird Nature Reserve, Changxing Qingcaosha Water Source Protection Area, Jiuduansha Wetland Nature Reserve, Jinshan Three Island Natural Reserve, and West Qingpu Dianshan Lake Wetland Restoration and Reconstruction Demonstration Area. The six wedges are the green land in Taopu, Dachang, Donggou, Zhangjiabang, Beicai and Sanlin. The 10 corridors are the 10 green corridors along high-capacity urban roads and along riversides. The multiple gardens are the parkland in the downtown area, and in new towns and new counties.

IV. Positively popularizing household garbage sorting and disposal

With a growing population, rapidly developing economy and improving living conditions, the amount of household garbage in Shanghai has kept on increasing. Since the 1990s, Shanghai has made positive explorations in promoting recycling, garbage sorting and urging manufacturers to reduce packaging, and in the light of these things, gradually established a system of sorting, collecting, transporting and disposing of garbage.

1. The sorting and decrement of household garbage in Shanghai

Sorting is a precondition to the efficient and quick disposal of garbage. Household garbage sorting in Shanghai was initiated in 1995, and since then there have been several adjustments to the categories, such as 'organic garbage, inorganic garbage, poisonous and harmful garbage'; 'dry garbage, wet garbage and harmful garbage'; 'waste glass, harmful garbage and combustible garbage'; 'compostable garbage, harmful garbage and other garbage'. Since 2007, Shanghai has started a four-type sorting mode of garbage. In residential areas, garbage is classified into 'harmful garbage, glass, recyclable garbage and other garbage'; in office areas such as in institutions or enterprises, garbage is classified into 'harmful garbage, recyclable garbage and other garbage'; in public places, garbage is classified into 'recyclable garbage and other garbage'; elsewhere, there is the separate disposal and distribution of garbage such as kitchen waste, bulky garbage, construction waste and disposable plastic lunch boxes.

To promote garbage sorting treatment, Shanghai in 2011 listed a project known as 'the low-carbon lifestyle of millions of families, garbage sorting being given priority' as an annual municipal government project, which involved Shanghai informing all households about the system of garbage sorted collection, sorted transport and sorted disposal. Such a project is oriented towards families, advocating garbage reduction, energy conservation and emission reduction, and a low-carbon lifestyle. It is aimed at popularizing the philosophy of garbage sorting to millions of families, by taking advantage of various entertainment educational activities, such as releasing information on the internet, knowledge contests, blogs and microblogs, and informing communities. Following the implementation of this project, the per capita disposal of household garbage in Shanghai experienced 'negative growth' for the first time in its history, with the per capita disposal of household garbage in the whole city decreasing by 5% compared with the previous year.

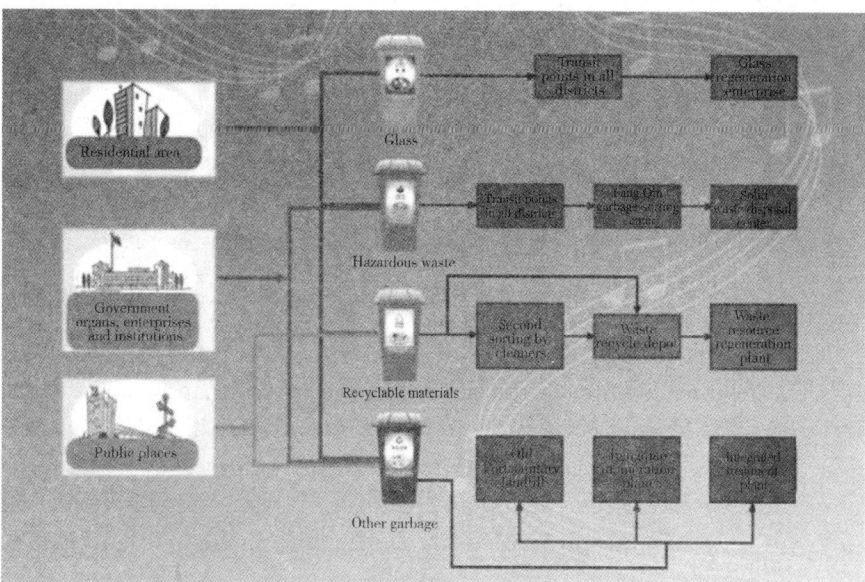

Figure 5-5 The sorting of household garbage in Shanghai

During the '12th five-year plan', Shanghai will gradually establish an overall sorting system of household garbage, encompassing dumping, collection and transportation, and disposal. In 2015, the per capita household garbage disposal was set to be controlled at around 0.8 kilogram a day, a fall of more than 20% compared with 2010.

2. The recycling and detoxification of Shanghai garbage disposal

(1) The recycling treatment of garbage. Shanghai has established a recycling system of renewable resources and a recycling institution of garbage sorting, so as to standardize the recycling, regeneration and utilization of sorted materials such as waste metals, waste paper, waste plastics and waste glass. Shanghai has also built recycling facilities for specific garbage categories such as construction garbage, bulky garbage, kitchen waste, and fallen branches

and leaves following afforestation. It has also promoted electricity generation through refuse incineration, the recycling and utilization of gas found in landfill sites, biotransformation, and the utilization of secondary resources such as methane and fly ash.

(2) The innocuity of garbage. The main measure is to establish waste treatment facilities where garbage may be sent to landfill, or incinerated or composted. Shanghai has systematically planned the layout of its garbage treatment facilities, and constructed a comprehensive utility base of solid waste in the Old Port of Shanghai, as well as garbage treatment facilities in the suburbs of Pudong and Jinshan. A household garbage collection, transportation and disposal system in rural areas has also been established, according to which 'garbage is dumped by individual households, collected by the village, transported by the town and disposed of by the district', with organic garbage disposed locally in the rural area.

As to the layout of garbage treatment facilities, during the '12th five-year plan' Shanghai has promoted the 'one major center with several small, comprehensive solid waste utility bases', propelling the construction of household garbage treatment facilities in the suburbs, and thus forming the three regional groups of 'the downtown area, suburban area and outer suburban area'. Household garbage in the downtown area is mainly disposed of by means of municipal facilities, and household garbage in the outer suburban area has access to an independent disposal system, while the suburban area and the downtown area will complement one another. In this way, a household garbage treatment pattern has been formed, which is oriented to multiple development through incineration and biochemical treatment, and which conforms to elementary sanitary standards.

Furthermore, Shanghai is still exploring the ecological renovation of dumping sites that have been closed, and plans to turn qualified sites into eco parks after restoration.

V. Exploring the ecological architecture concept

Sustainable development is a universal theme of the 21st century. Urban architecture is supposed to be transformed from a high-consumption development mode to a high-efficiency ecological development mode. Ecological architecture integrates itself with human beings and the natural environment, and as an important part of sustainable development, it represents a global architectural development trend. Shanghai attaches great importance to the construction of ecological architecture, and has carried out a series of designs and explorations, conducting various demonstration projects and achieving some significant research achievements.

> **Column 5-2 What is ecological architecture?**
>
> Ecological architecture follows the principle of sustainable development, and is oriented by high and new technology and targeted at all links in the architecture life cycle, for the purpose of creating an environment characterized by high efficiency, low consumption, no-waste and no-pollution, health and comfort, and ecological balance, by means of scientific integrated design. Such ecological architecture may improve the functions, efficiency and comfort, representing an ecological philosophy of resource conservation, energy saving, environmental protection and people orientation, which may fully show the harmony between architecture and humanity, environment and technology.

1. Shanghai demonstration building of ecological architecture

Shanghai demonstration building of ecological architecture is located in Shanghai Xinzhuang industrial zone. Designed by Shanghai Research Institute of Building Science, it has a building area of 1,900 square meters. This demonstration building is also the fruit of Shanghai's major scientific research project 'the key technology research of ecological architecture and system integration', which was China's first real demonstration building of ecological architecture.

A long list of new technologies and new products are employed in Shanghai's demonstration buildings of ecological architecture, such as the four types of exterior wall insulation system, the three types of sun-shading systems, heat-proof aluminum alloy LOW-E windows with double glazing and cavity in the middle, sunshine control film, natural ventilation systems, new-type air conditioning systems with independent control over heat and humidity, solar air conditioners, underfloor heating systems, solar photovoltaic power generation grid connection techniques, rain water and sewage recycling techniques, recycling aggregate concrete technique, intelligent indoor environment regulatory system, afforestation configuration system, ecological maintenance of the landscaped water area, the ecological restoration system, single-layer drainage system, and environment-friendly materials for decoration. By matching design and application with architecture integration, some technical features are well represented, such as natural ventilation, ultralow energy consumption, natural illumination, healthy air conditioning, renewable energy, green building materials, intelligent control, resource recycling, ecological afforestation and a comfortable environment. Intelligent control may be taken as an example. The building is endowed with 'intelligence' and 'facial expressions', and once it is crowded with people and the carbon dioxide content rises, a sensor will automatically 'notify' a window that will let fresh air in, with the frequency of ventilation occurring as often as several dozen times per hour.

The utilization of multiple ecological technologies enable the comprehensive energy consumption of the demonstration building to be just one quarter of the building of a similar type, and the renewable energy utilization rate accounts for 20% of architecture energy consumption, with the renewable resources utility rate reaching 60%. The indoor environment satisfies health and comfort standards, which represents the basic philosophy of ecological architecture, which stresses 'saving resources, protecting the environment and being people-oriented'.

2. Chenjia town demonstration building with super-low energy consumption

Chenjia town demonstration building with super-low energy consumption is located in Shanghai Chongming county, with a building area of 5,117 square meters. Such a demonstration building is designed by following the sustainable concept, and it is a green building with super-low energy consumption, in terms of low carbon emissions, energy-saving and cost-reduction, and the recycling of resources. The pilot demonstration building employs 10 ecological techniques, including climate adaptation-type building energy-saving technology, compound-type air conditioning technology, collaborative utility of solar energy and wind energy technology, technology to improve natural ventilation, individualized fresh air technology, technology to improve the efficiency of natural lighting, high-efficiency resource recycling utility technology, urine and feces separation and collection technology, technology that can realize passive energy conservation by intelligent means, and technologies that imitate natural ecological forests and foster biological diversity. Such a building has five highlights: a comprehensive architecture energy conservation above 75%; a renewable energy utility rate of more than 50%; a renewable resource utility rate of above 60%; zero consumption can be realized in the process of operation (the amount of new energy generated annually by the building is approximately equal to that consumed annually); and zero emission can be realized in the process of operation (inorganic refuse such as waste paper and waste plastics can be recycled and utilized by means of the salvage of waste material, and organic refuse is completely recycled in the building's yard).

3. The ecological architectural concept and technology employed in Shanghai World Expo

In the architectural design and plan of China 2010 Shanghai World Expo, the concept and technology of ecological architecture were fully employed and exhibited, which inspired visitors and made them yearn for the popularization of future ecological architecture as they visited and experienced the demonstration of the ecological architecture.

(1) Integrated solar energy utilization The Theme Pavilion of Shanghai World Expo was largely covered by integrated solar panels, and with an installed solar-powered generating capacity of 2.87MW connected to the grid, the generated solar power could be transmitted back to the urban grid. In addition, the 'magic box ecological house', 'BedZED ecological house' and 'Madrid public housing area' in the urban best practices area all employed a solar energy collection system, fully utilizing solar energy as the source of energy.

(2) The ecological landscape combining beauty with function At the 2010 Shanghai World Expo China Pavilion, a small-scale constructed wetland was incorporated into the landscape design, and as the ecological landscape, it may realize self-cleaning by circulation. On the outer walls of the east and west sides of the theme pavilion, there was an extra layer of vertical plants covering 7,000 square meters, which may have the dual functions of heat retention and thermal insulation in summer. The musée du quai Branly-Jacques Chirac in the urban best practices area adopted 'plant wall' technology that not only realized the functions of ventilation, irrigation and heat insulation, but also contained a large variety of plants, thus having great ornamental value.

(3) The sound technological integration system 'Shanghai eco housing' in the urban best practices area claimed to 'integrate the latest technology'. For instance, the housing ventilation, lighting and air-conditioning systems were all automatically adjusted according to the weather conditions and people's true feelings. Inside the eco house, the light guiding system allowed sunlight to enter the north room, while the transparent glass ceiling in the atrium was equipped with flexible opening angles, which meant that in the daytime the lights need not be turned on.

Chapter 6

The Operation and Administration of Shanghai City

As an extra-large city, Shanghai faces many problems in its operation, and has to meet high standards in administration philosophy, administration system and administration methods. During years of exploration, Shanghai has established an efficient system of administration for an extra-large city operation, accumulating valuable experience in the city administration system mechanism, optimization of city transportation, food safety guarantees, prevention and reduction of natural disasters, and urban appearance management, which could be used as a reference by other cities.

I. Exploring and promoting the devolution of the city administration focus

Under the planned economic system, Shanghai's city administration was highly centralized in municipal administrative departments. The positivity and initiative of districts and counties were not fully realized, and so the grassroots were not actively involved in administration. Since the mid-1990s, Shanghai has gradually explored a more scientific way to conduct city administration, and in 1996 it officially put forward a 'two-level government, three-level administration' system framework in urban areas and a 'three-level government, three-level administration' system framework in suburban areas, promoting the devolution of the administrative center. After many years of exploration and effort, Shanghai has established a system mechanism and corresponding working mechanism of an extra-large city hierarchical management administration, which involve 'two-level government (three-level in suburban areas), three-level administration and four-level network'. The two-level government refers to the municipal government and district governments, and since the sub-district offices represent district governments and are thus included in the 'two-level government', they are not only the executors of government policies, but also the pivots coordinating political, economic and cultural activities. The three-level government in suburban areas refers to the county government, town government and village government, and three-level administration refers to the municipal government's top-down administration mode, to district governments and then to sub-district offices, with sub-district offices supervising neighborhood committees and dealing with most community affairs through the committees.

1. Delegating the office authority of city administration

In the exploratory stage, the main task was to adjust the labor division between the municipal and district governments, and to promote the devolution of office authority of the municipal government to district governments, including house planning, land development, residential property, municipal administration, environmental sanitation and garden management. The division of responsibility between the municipal government and district governments was well defined, and so the framework of hierarchical management took elementary shape. After the official launching of the reform of the government's hierarchical management system, municipal departments further delegated the office authority of planning and public facilities administration, laying emphasis on reinforcing the authority and functions of sub-district offices, which were granted four rights: urban planning participation rights just for the district in which the sub-district was based, hierarchical management, comprehensive coordination power and localization management. Sub-district offices also took measures to establish an integrated enforcement team, strengthening the authorized size of sub-district offices and neighborhood committees, and improving the financial resources mechanism. Sub-district offices also took responsibility for implementing these measures. In addition, the sub-district system was also reformed to promote the separation of government functions from enterprise management, office authority and community management. As a result, some routine functions that were originally fulfilled by sub-district offices were separated, such as the community service, community culture, employment and market management, and then various kinds of professional facilitating agencies were established, which contributed to the formation of a city administration pattern of 'small government, big society'.

2. Establishing the comprehensive law enforcement system mechanism

In the process of promoting the hierarchical management of government, sub-district supervisory brigades were set up in the city's 100 sub-districts, implementing integrated law enforcement in a simplified way. Thereafter, Shanghai further promoted city administration integrated law enforcement reform, thus forming a comparatively complete comprehensive law enforcement system and network at the city, district and sub-district level. Comprehensive law enforcement was carried out at the district level, and the district-level city administration supervisory brigade was responsible for the implementation of integrated law enforcement in environmental sanitation, road administration, afforestation and sub-district supervision. The Municipal Law Enforcement Bureau of City Administration was responsible for unified guidance, coordination and supervision of law enforcement across the whole city, and the municipal general brigade was in charge of the operational guidance of those brigades in all districts.

3. Establishing an urban grid administration system mechanism

Shanghai started to establish an urban grid administration mode in 2005. Grid administration, centering on information technology and based on grid-like areas, was designed to promote the timely discovery of city administration problems, followed by a quick response and efficient solution, by means of the grid administration information platform. The key points cover the following four aspects. The first was to digitalize administrative subjects, divide administrative areas into a 10,000-square meter unit grid (by taking into consideration original housing estates and original administrative divisions), and unifying the coding and forming a uniform electronic map of the whole city. In addition, urban administration residents, companies and other subjects were uniformly represented by unit and event and uniformly classified and coded, accompanied by their clear names, classifications and property illustrations. In this way, a uniform unit and event database was formed in the city, with each district having a back-up copy of its own data. The second key point was to network the information process. Supervisors took advantage of the 'integrated networking facility for city administration' to collect on-the-spot information (picture, character and sound files) and then, through wireless networks, transmit them to a supervising center or receive orders from the supervising center. The third was to establish a supervision platform. The municipal supervising platform is in charge of analysis, supervision and appraisal, transmitting the collected information to the district platform, directing and coordinating the specialized municipal department and the district platform of supervision and appraisal. The district supervision platform is responsible for discovering problems, supervision, coordination, disposal and verification. The fourth key point was that, at the municipal and district levels, the city administration supervision and management functions were separated, and the supervising center and command center were established. The municipal supervising center is responsible for information transmission and analysis and appraisal, while the municipal command center is in charge of commanding and coordinating the specialized municipal department to tackle related problems.

II. Implementing a 'public transport priority' strategy

In order to solve traffic jams in an extra-large city, Shanghai has implemented a strategy of giving priority to urban public transport, constantly improving the convenience, reliability and comfort of public transport to facilitate the movement of citizens, and promoting the harmonious development between public transport and the economy.

1. Improving public transport infrastructure

First of all, rail transit construction needs to be promoted with utmost effort. By the end of 2012, there were 11 rail transit lines with 285 stations (including nine shared stations), with an operational mileage of 428km, more than any other world city, including Tokyo and New York. Second, the construction of transfer hubs and public transport stations has been accelerated. Up to now, as many as 60 comprehensive transfer hubs have been established, and some of them have 'park and ride' facilities. Third, a large-capacity bus rapid transit system has been developed. In combination with the transformation of its road network and the construction of expressways, rapid bus transit lines have been established, with an emphasis on creating passenger transport corridors and major roads linking urban and rural areas. Fourth, bus lanes have been developed. Great effort has been exerted on constructing bus lanes in downtown areas, in new towns and suburban areas, and lanes that link urban areas with rural areas. As a result, the speed and punctuality of public transport have improved. Currently, Shanghai has 160km of public transit lanes, and in addition, since the roads are either newly built or rebuilt, harbor-like bus stops along the public transit lanes were also constructed. In accordance with the construction of large-scale public facilities, supportive harbor-like taxi stands have also been constructed in order to improve traffic operation efficiency. To further guarantee the smooth running of public transport, Shanghai has made improvements to some road sections where public transport lanes or bus lanes overlap to promote the optimal construction of traffic signals and improve signal systems.

Figure 6-1 Shanghai bus lane (photograph by Chen Fei, Xinhua News Agency)

2. Implementing the connection of public transport and the preferential transfer of public transport

Shanghai attaches great importance to connecting different modes of public transport. In order to maximize convenience for its citizens, Shanghai promotes the connection between different rail lines, and between rail transport and ground public transport, in terms of operation scheduling, information sign improvements and preferential fares for transport interchange. Passengers using different types of public transport can take advantage of preferential transfer fares. The 'preferential fares for transport interchange' policy was initiated in 2006, and it includes the following measures. On air-conditioned buses that operate on preferential routes, passengers are entitled to a preferential fare of Rmb1 per journey so long as the interchange happens within 90 minutes. Passengers using the same transportation card may be entitled to a preferential fare of Rmb1 to interchange from rail transit to air-conditioned bus, or vice versa, within 90 minutes. Passengers whose rail transit costs exceed Rmb70 a month may be entitled to a 10% rail discount during that month, thus enjoying two privileges. Senior citizens over 70 years old are entitled to a special preferential rail and bus fare during off-peak hours, and to free rides all day during holidays and festivals. In 2009, Shanghai came up with further measures to expand interchange benefits, so as to cover all public transport lines and all vehicles in city, with the preferential interchange time increasing from 90 minutes to two hours.

3. Promoting the informatization of public transport

Shanghai continues to promote the development of an intelligent public transport system, and with the full employment of information technology, has established an operation supervision information system that, by taking stations as network nodes and vehicles as information terminals, transmits real-time operation information, carries out intelligent dispatch and improves operational efficiency. Specific measures include equipping public buses with vehicle-mounted, real-time location devices, and in certain bus stations setting up electronic bus information boards; establishing a comprehensive transportation hub network platform to share information, and setting up a public transport operation information release and inquiry service system for passengers on the move, so as to collect real-time operation information and provide information services on bus routes, thus realizing the target of intelligentized dispatch.

III. Attaching great importance to food safety administration

In recent years, Shanghai has attached great importance to food safety administration and has improved the administration system mechanism, striving to build Shanghai as one of the safest cities in China in terms of food integrity.

1. Establishing and improving the food safety administration system

Shanghai Municipal Food Safety Committee and its offices have a number of member institutions, including Shanghai Agriculture Committee, Shanghai Administration for Industry and Commerce, Shanghai Municipal Bureau of Quality and Technical Supervision, Shanghai Municipal Food and Drug Administration, Shanghai Entry-Exit Inspection and Quarantine Bureau, Shanghai Municipal Public Security Bureau, the Department of Propaganda of Shanghai Municipal Party Committee, Shanghai Municipal Development and Reform Commission, Shanghai Economy and Information Technology Commission, Shanghai Municipal Commission of Commerce, Shanghai Municipal Health Bureau, Shanghai Municipal Finance Bureau, Shanghai Environmental Protection Bureau, Shanghai Bureau of Afforestation, Shanghai Municipal Supervision Bureau, Shanghai Administration of Grain, the Legislative Affairs Office of Shanghai municipal people's government and the

Information Office of Shanghai municipality. Between these departments, there are well defined working responsibilities and supervising duties, and corresponding coordination and adjudication systems were established.[1] At the district and county level, there are also food safety committees and their offices, conducting their own substantial food safety coordination operations, and organizing the joint inspection of major events and the comprehensive coordination of major affairs. In all towns (sub-districts), the food safety comprehensive coordination agencies are well established so as to reinforce grassroots supervision. In addition, governments at all levels put their respective supervision responsibilities into effect, and those in charge, from the municipal to district (county) level and town (sub-district) level, and then further to the village (neighborhood) committee, are all required to be responsible for food safety. Their work on food safety is also taken into consideration in a government's performance assessment. In 2013, the whole city initiated the institutional reform of food and drug supervision, and the offices in the departments of industry and commerce and quality inspection that are related to food safety supervision were transferred to be in charge of Shanghai Municipal Food and Drug Administration, which contributes to bringing about the change of food safety supervision from 'multiple management' to 'single management'.

2. Formulating and perfecting local regulations, rules and standards

The local legislative work of food safety is forcefully promoted, and a series of local regulations, rules and normative documents has been formed (see Table 6-1), which provide a powerful guarantee for food safety supervision. Shanghai has also enhanced the formulation and revision of local standards for food safety, and the Municipal Food and Drug Administration has set up a review committee on Shanghai's standards for food safety, and has come up with 18 local standards that provide forceful support for the supervision.

3. Carrying out the specific program of addressing food safety problems

Shanghai has organized several specific programs to address food safety problems, including cracking down on the illegal addition of non-food

---

[1] http://www.spaq.sh.cn/gb/node2/spaq/index.html, November 18, 2012

substances and the abuse of food additives, guaranteeing quality safety of dairy products, addressing waste cooking oils and fats and cooking waste, and guaranteeing the safety of meat, health foods and alcoholic drinks. Shanghai public security departments have taken the lead in organizing a crackdown that is designed to fight against the crimes that endanger food and drug safety, and have organized other inspection departments, thus forming a cohesive mechanism of execution. The targets are 'black dens', where food is produced without a qualifying certificate or license, as well as the illegal application of pesticides and the veterinary drug Clenbuterol, and the illegal slaughter of animals. A total of 8,037 food safety cases have been filed, resulting in 80 criminal prosecutions. In this way, a high-pressure situation has been formed in which illegal food production and operation is under strict control.

Table 6-1 General survey of Shanghai's 2011 local regulations on food safety

Category	Name
Local regulation	Shanghai Measures for the Implementation of The Food Safety Law of the PRC
Government regulations	Shanghai Regulations on Pig Products Quality Safety Supervision
	Shanghai Regulations on the Granting of Permits to Individual Food Producers
	Shanghai Regulations on Catering Service Permits
Normative documents	Shanghai Municipal People's Government Decision on Establishing Shanghai Municipal Food Safety Committee
	On Further Reinforcing the Work of Food Safety in Shanghai
	On Implementing the Further Reinforcement of the Strict Supervision and Administration of Kitchen Waste Oils and Fats in Shanghai
	On Implementing the Further Reinforcement of Awards for Reporting on Shanghai Food Safety
	On Further Reinforcing the Food Safety Work in the Field of Distribution

4. Improving the risk assessment mechanism of food safety

Shanghai takes measures in reinforcing the organization and implementation of risk monitoring, improving the risk monitoring network and initiating foodborne disease monitoring. An expert committee of food safety risk assessment has been established, which is composed of experts in the fields of medical science, agriculture, food and nutrition. There are more than 100 risk monitoring sampling sites and more than 10 contract labs that are engaged in the laboratory testing of risk monitoring samples. Such testing covers all kinds of food, and by statistical analysis can analyze what food may incur the greatest social harm, and consequently, emphasis would be placed on the testing of that food. For those issues that are of the greatest concern for society, risk monitoring and assessment will be carried out, and exchanging information on the risks should be actively promoted so that the risk monitoring analysis results are reported to the higher authority, and notified to related supervision departments, trade associations and chain outlets. On the basis of the result of risk monitoring, a special information bulletin will be compiled. In the future, Shanghai will also gradually establish a risk monitoring network 'from farmland to dining table' that covers the entire food chain.

5. Adopting the technological supervision approach

Shanghai popularizes the utilization of on-site rapid testing techniques, promotes the establishment and application of a food safety traceability system, boosts food safety supervision and the establishment of an information service platform, and integrates the resources of food safety testing and detection. In addition, Shanghai also encourages food production enterprises to establish their own inspection body, which contributes to the formation of a food safety inspection system that combines the government, society and enterprises.

6. Improving the major event emergency mechanism of food safety

The administrative department formulates an emergency disposal system for major food safety incidents, drawing up pre-arranged planning procedures for emergencies, and in striving to eliminate all hidden dangers of food safety, thus addressing a series of major events in a timely and efficient manner. In addition, the government attaches importance to responding to public sentiment and the release of food safety information, establishing a systematic mechanism for monitoring, collecting, analyzing and addressing public sentiment. The government has also established a news spokesman system to reinforce communication with the media, and to release food safety information without delay and respond to the concerns of society and the media.

IV. Making and implementing plans to prevent and reduce disasters

Shanghai is a city prone to many natural disasters such as typhoons, heavy rains and spring tide, and to many urban accidents such as power cuts and fires that are also big threats to people's lives and properties and the city's overall development. In recent years, Shanghai has enhanced the work of preventing and reducing disasters, intensifying the implementation of a national comprehensive disaster prevention and reduction plan, so that the security of city operations can be efficiently guaranteed.

1. Establishing a disaster prevention and reduction linkage mechanism across multiple departments

Shanghai has established a linkage mechanism across the departments of meteorology, flood prevention, health, food and drug supervision, and civil administration, which has improved the efficiency of urban prevention and reduction of disasters. For instance, in the event of cold weather, the meteorological department will release timely preventative information, and then departments such as the Economy and Information Technology Commission will be responsible for ensuring the supply of electricity, gas, water, coal, heating and oil. Other departments such as public transportation, public security and municipal administration will use vehicles that have back-up fuel tanks, reinforcing the security and safety of roads, especially expressways; housing department will carry out safety and freeze-prevention checks in old-style houses; the press department will release disaster forecasts and advice on self-preservation and self-rescue; the municipal emergency office in cooperation with the meteorological department will bring together some related institutions to formulate and improve concrete plans.

2. Reinforcing the construction of natural disaster monitoring and early warning appraisal capabilities

Shanghai has gradually constructed a social security warning network covering a wide range, including information forecast systems on public hygiene and epidemic prevention, meteorology, earthquakes and floods. Some major industries and enterprises closely related to public security are also exploring the establishment of a constant warning information system, so that they could collect, analyze, discriminate and identify potential risks, and make scientific predictions of the nature, magnitude and range of the risk, as well as when and where it may occur, and then make the timely release of warning information. During the '12th five-year plan', Shanghai will establish 200 community risk appraisal demonstration spots, and then formulate a risk map of the whole city. In the meantime, on the basis of GIS spatial information system, a community risk appraisal system will be established to realize the sharing of comprehensive risk information, which may provide technical support to the prevention plan and coping strategy.

3. Enhancing the regional and grassroots capabilities of disaster prevention and reduction

Over the years, Shanghai has kept reinforcing the strength of urban buildings and public facilities, enhancing the disaster prevention and reduction capabilities of infrastructure such as urban and rural transportation, communications, radio and television, civil air defense, electric power, gas and water supply, the sewage system, schools and hospitals. Shanghai also constructs or renovates urban public emergency infrastructure and evacuation shelters, making full use of facilities such as civil air defense guidance, alerts, projects, and evacuation to provide guarantees for emergency administration, public security and safety of the masses. For instance, in Dalian Road greenbelt, Shanghai has established its first municipal-level emergency shelter. This greenbelt is a place of leisure, recreation and fitness for citizens in ordinary times, but in the case of disasters such as earthquake, emergency lavatories, drinking water and power supply could be initiated within three-to-four hours. There is also a helipad in the greenbelt, equipped with an emergency command system. The greenbelt can accommodate 6,000 persons taking refuge for a period of more than 30 days.

4. Establishing an emergency mechanism for urban security

Shanghai has established a full coverage emergency administration network that combines 'strip, block and spot'. The municipal civil administration, safety supervision, health and public security bureaus are in charge of the promotion of emergency management covering, respectively, natural disasters, accidents, public health and public security. The Municipal Civil Affairs Bureau, Shanghai Municipal Education Commission and Shanghai Administration of Work Safety are, respectively, responsible for promoting emergency administration in communities, schools and enterprises. An emergency response mechanism has been established, with levels and types clearly classified. Shanghai Municipal Emergency Linkage Center is responsible for the command and dispatch of 27 units such as health, water supply, gas and electric power. In times of grave emergency, the first department on the scene will carry out initial work until the arrival of the professional department. In addition, an emergency plan system has been constructed; the legal foundation has been improved; the building of an emergency rescue team has been reinforced; and the emergency administration capabilities of urban security has been constantly upgraded.

5. Improving the social mobilization capability of preventing and reducing disasters

Shanghai has improved the social mobilization mechanism of disaster prevention and reduction, expedited channels for members of society to participate in disaster prevention and reduction, formulated policies and measures encouraging enterprises, non-governmental organizations and volunteers to participate in disaster prevention and reduction, thereby creating a favorable atmosphere in which all of society are actively involved in disaster prevention and reduction. For instance, in the 2012 'Day of Disaster Prevention and Reduction' series of activities, Shanghai organized a variety of community activities rich in content, diversified propaganda campaigns, and training and education activities on the theme of disaster prevention and reduction.

V. Reinforcing the administration and maintenance of the urban appearance

1. Establishing a localized administration system

Shanghai attaches great importance to the reform of its urban appearance administration system, and has taken the lead nationally in carrying out the comprehensive reform of its appearance and environmental sanitation. The priority of the reform is to rechart the responsibility divisions between the municipal and district (county) level, with many assignments delegated to the districts (counties), such as the reduction of household garbage, the cleaning up of rivers and waterways, the disposal of waste soil and vehicle cleaning. The fund that used to be controlled by the municipal finance departments has been delegated to the districts (counties). As a result, the construction of administrative departments in districts (counties) has been further improved, with executive agencies established to deal with administrative affairs. At the sub-district, town and village levels, the administrative agencies in charge of the city's appearance and environmental sanitation have been gradually established, which effectively promotes the delegation of administrative priorities.[2]

---

[2] *Experiences of the Comprehensive Reform of City Appearance and Environmental Sanitation – and the Trade Reform of Shanghai's City Appearance and Environmental Sanitation*, January, 22, 2009

2. Introducing the marketized operation mechanism

Shanghai adheres to the marketization operation mechanism in the administration and maintenance of the city's appearance and environment, and introduces various types of capital into the construction and maintenance of environmental sanitation facilities, thus forming a pattern of multiple investment, financing and repayment, multi-participation and international cooperation. The service market bodies are actively fostered, and the environmental sanitation service units are undergoing a thorough transformation from public institution system to enterprise system. Other market bodies have also been introduced into the environmental sanitation market. The service market is largely encouraged to open up, accompanied by the implementation of a government procurement system and public bidding and tendering system in the construction and maintenance of infrastructure. A reasonable price system has been established, and social enterprises are encouraged and allowed to enter into all the fields of the environmental sanitation service industry, so that various market bodies might be attracted to join the construction and operation market of urban appearance and environmental sanitation.

> **Column 6-1 Marketization of maintenance operation**
>
> In 2013, the municipal government issued *Guidelines on Further Deepening the Marketization Reform of Shanghai Urban Maintenance Operation*, so as to accelerate the transformation of government functions and clarify the relationship between the government and enterprises in terms of maintenance operation, and thus further promoting the maintenance marketization process of road facilities, city afforestation, drainage and waterways. Shanghai City Afforestation Administration and the afforestation departments in all districts and counties study and formulate concrete implementation plans of the marketization reform of the maintenance of city afforestation, based on the actual situation in their own areas. Pilot projects include Changning Afforestation Administration and Gongqing Forest Park.

3. Establishing the price system and standard system of urban appearance and environmental sanitation services

Shanghai formulated the *Guide Price for Shanghai's Environmental Sanitation Public Service Project*, working out price quotas for Shanghai's city appearance and environmental sanitation maintenance. Shanghai has also accelerated the construction of environmental sanitation quality standards, issuing trade technical specifications such as *Shanghai Specifications for Public Lavatory Cleaning Services*, *Shanghai Specifications for Urban Road Sweeping and Cleaning*, *Operation Guidelines for Cleaning Public Squares and Sidewalks (Preliminary version)* and *Shanghai Specifications for City Appearance Standard*.

4. Reinforcing the administration of the urban appearance and environment quality supervision

Shanghai has established a linkage mechanism of city appearance and environment quality supervision, and formed the principle of 'timely discovery, quick response, efficient solution and powerful supervision'. Quality supervision agencies have been established in all districts and counties to conduct supervision and administration of the urban appearance and environment. Shanghai has also constructed two information systems to further improve the efficiency of supervision and administration of the urban appearance and environment. One is the transmission platform of quality supervision information, which is open to all quality supervision agencies as well as sub-district supervision stations in the 18 districts and counties. This has contributed to the realization of quality supervision information sharing. The other is the information management system of the urban appearance and environment quality supervision, integrating historical management data, dynamic supervision information, management content, management items and management standards into an integrated information platform.

Chapter 7

The Development Prospects of Shanghai

Looking to the future, Shanghai stands at another new starting point. From the perspectives of economic scale, industrial structure and city function, Shanghai will enter a new stage in terms of economy, society and urban development. Under these circumstances, Shanghai has to break away from its former development route and use innovation to stimulate urban transformation and development. It needs to improve its urban functions and realize new breakthroughs by deepening reform in all directions, optimizing the urban spatial layout, developing strategic emerging industries, and building an international cultural metropolis and a world-famous tourist city.

I. A global city with the capacity of global resource allocation

With the constant deepening of urbanization across the world, cities are playing an increasingly important role in the global economic network, and competition between countries will gradually evolve into competition between cities. In the coming 30 years, China will remain in the phase where its economy grows rapidly, and will be committed to the realization of the China Dream that envisions a wealthy, powerful and rejuvenated country, and the people being contented and happy. As China plays a more conspicuous role in the world economy, there is an urgent need for global cities with the capacity of global resource allocation to represent China to participate in international competition.[1] Shanghai is located in the pivot of the chain of modern cities along the coast of east Asia, and it shoulders the responsibilities of participating in and influencing world economic affairs, fulfilling the role of an important spatial carrier of the flow and allocation

---

[1] The global city is referred to as the main (basic) node city in the global city network system, and it is the control and administrative center of the global network

of global economic resources, and getting involved in the reorganization of the international economic order through its influence and network control power, which bears a paramount strategic significance to realizing the great rejuvenation of the Chinese nation.

1. The strategic target is to become a major network node in the world city network system

In the global city network system, the intensity of mutual connections affect the energy level of the city node. For a burgeoning city like Shanghai, the key lies in the creation of a larger economic flow and larger and more efficient resource allocation space, through the deep integration into the world city network and the establishment of wide economic connections with the outside, for the purpose of improving the capability of mobilizing and allocating resources. Therefore, Shanghai's basic target orientation in the construction of a global city is, on the basis of network and intensification, to drastically improve the energy level of the city network node, reinforce the function of global coordination, provide a large platform for the circulation and allocation of global resource factors, and provide a friendly interface for the circulation of resource factors between Shanghai and the world so that it can play a key role in the development of the global economy and culture.

2. The core task is to build a global network platform

For Shanghai to become a major network node in the global network economy, it must build a network platform with global resource allocation capabilities.

(1) Agglomerating functional agencies. To build a global network platform, Shanghai needs to make the essential step of agglomerating functional agencies such as transnational enterprises, large-scale global service companies and international organizations. The increase in the number and scale of functional agencies and the deepening connections with the outside world may contribute to the enlargement of the connection scope with the outside world, an increase in the number of network nodes and the expansion of the network platform and its flow.

(2) Focusing on accelerating the expansion of freight flow. On the basis of real conditions, Shanghai is focusing on building a global network platform to expand the flow, especially the freight flow, so as to mobilize and accelerate the flow speed of a variety of factors, and to improve the global

coordination function. Years ahead, another phase may be reached in which the network platform and its flow are expanded and the capital flow may play the dominant role.

3. The building path is to construct a strategic system with five dimensions

(1) The opening-up orientation strategy. Shanghai will take the historic opportunity of building China (Shanghai) Pilot Free Trade Zone to further upgrade the opening-up strategy, reinforce the breadth and depth of opening up, enhance foreign investment, promote the free and orderly flow of economic factors both at home and abroad, the efficient allocation of resources, and the deep integration of the market, and accelerate the fostering of new strength in participating in and leading international economic cooperation to upgrade its globalization.

(2) The service orientation strategy. The industrial development orientation and guideline for Shanghai to build a global city is to upgrade its industrial energy level, and focus on the development of a modern service sector and advanced manufacturing industry under a service economy framework. Shanghai is also to build a new type of industrial system that is high-end, intensified and service-oriented, so as to promote the development of a service economy that is based on industrial integration. Domestically, Shanghai will focus on the transformation from aid service, in which it supplies money and technical support, to radiation service; internationally, Shanghai will build a service system that serves globalized production, and fosters the provision of professional services and the production base of financial innovation products and production factors.

(3) The regional interaction strategy. The global urban region[2] has come to be the regional basis for global city development; therefore Shanghai, as a rising global city, must rely on the rising of its surrounding area. Currently, the Yangtze River Delta is the region in China that most closely bears the feature of a global urban region, with the cities in this region all bearing a high level of globalization. On the basis of improving and implementing the Yangtze River Delta regional plan, Shanghai actively promotes the integration of the Yangtze River Delta and is building a global urban region to boost the overall competitiveness of the region.

---

[2] The global city and it adjacent hinterland establish a close inner link that contributes to the forming of a global urban region

(4) The network expansion strategy. To integrate into the global city node system, Shanghai will take freight flow as the phasal focus, striving to implement a development strategy oriented by network flow expansion to further accelerate the integrated development of capital flow, information flow and freight flow. Shanghai will also make efforts to attract the settling of multinational enterprises and foster local transnational enterprises, and vigorously implement a strategy of enterprises 'going global' and accelerate building the node status of the global products production chain.

(5) The talent agglomeration strategy. Sticking to the guideline of taking talent as the first resource, and with an eye to the need to build global city functions, Shanghai vigorously fosters and agglomerates professional talents, with a focus on the innovation of talent working mechanism and the perfection of a talent policy system. Shanghai will gradually implement the market allocation and contractualization administration of talents, in order to foster a favorable environment to attract top-level specialists to work in the city, and to build leading global talent.

II. Comprehensively deepening reform and improving the city administration system

The third plenary session of the 18th Central Committee of the CPC put forward the strategic target of developing socialism with Chinese characteristics, and improving the state administration system and administration capability. As the bellwether of China's reform and opening up, Shanghai set about constructing the city administration system, comprehensively deepening reform, and constantly reaping the benefits of reform and opening up. In the light of the plenary session, improving the city administration system means building and improving, under the leadership of the party, a whole set of closely connected and mutually coordinated systems such as the system mechanism, the law and regulations, in a myriad of fields such as the economy, politics, culture, society, ecological civilization and party construction. Shanghai's comprehensive deepening reform and improving the city administration system may cover the following six key tasks.

1. Constructing a socialist market economy system that is unified and open, competitive and orderly, fair and effective

Shanghai will make the market play a key role in resource allocation, on the basis of which the city will deepen economic system reform. Shanghai will also stick to and improve the basic economic system, accelerate the perfection of a modern market system, macro-regulation system and open economic system, accelerate the construction of an innovative society, and promote a more efficient, fairer and more sustainable economic development.

2. Constructing a highly transparent and highly efficient modern administrative system

Shanghai will center on the target of creating a highly transparent and efficient service; fewer examining processes and charges; respecting the market law and the creative spirit of the people, further deepening the reform of the administrative system and mechanism, and promoting government functional transformation. Focusing on institutional supply, macro regulation, social service, market order maintenance and public administration, Shanghai will reduce its interference in microeconomic activities and gradually transfer and reduce its administrative power, giving part of the market back to the market competition mechanism so as to activate market vitality. Shanghai will also reinforce the public service and administration functions, simplify the process of examination and approval before the event, and enhance supervision during and after the event, normalizing the supervision activities.

3. Constructing the cultural system mechanism that is open and accommodating, diversified and competitive

Shanghai will center on the construction of a socialist cultural metropolis and deepen the reform of the cultural system mechanism, sticking to the main thread of marketization reform of cultural industries, vigorously accelerating the perfection of the cultural administration system and cultural production and operation mechanism, expanding cultural marketization and the pace of opening up, establishing and improving the modern public cultural service system and modern cultural market system, and promoting the development and prosperity of socialist culture.

4. Constructing a social administration system that improves people's livelihoods, practices fairness and justice, and involves multiple participation

Centering on better guaranteeing and improving people's livelihoods and promoting social fairness and justice, Shanghai will deepen social system reform, reform the income distribution system, promote collective prosperity, promote system innovation in the social field, boost the equalization of public services, establish the urban and rural development integration system and mechanism that involves equal participation and joint sharing, accelerate the creation of a scientific and efficient social administration system, and guarantee the full vitality, harmony and order of society.

5. Constructing an ecological civilization system that is complete and linked across districts

Centering on the construction of a beautiful city, Shanghai will deepen ecological civilization system reform, accelerate the construction of ecological civilization system, perfect the system and mechanism of spatial exploitation of national land, resource conservation and employment, and ecological environment protection.

6. Constructing a party construction system that is scientific, democratic and adheres to the rule of law

Centering on the improvement of scientific, democratic and legal administration by the state, Shanghai will deepen party construction system reform by reinforcing the system of democratic centralism, perfecting the system by which leading cadres directly contact and serve the masses, improving the system of writing style and the common practice at meetings, perfecting the system of hard work and plain living, improving the system of selecting and appointing cadres, and reforming the government performance evaluation system, so that the party can fulfil its role in considering all situations and coordinating all parties.

III. 'Innovation driving development, economic transformation being upgraded'

Since the 1990s, Shanghai has followed the extensive development mode, by which it mainly relies on large amounts of capital investment, low labor costs and large consumption of land and resources. As the bottlenecks of land, cost and environment grow more and more conspicuous, together with the intensification of international market demands and a change in international industrial specialization brought about by the technological revolution, Shanghai put forward the strategy of 'innovation driving development, economic transformation being upgraded', laying a solid foundation for long-term development.[3]

---

[3] *Innovation as Impetus for Transformation and Development – 2010/2011 Shanghai Development Report*, Shanghai: Truth and Wisdom Press, 2011

1. The profound connotations of 'innovation driving development, economic transformation being upgraded'

The strategy of 'innovation driving development, economic transformation being upgraded' is centered on a transformation that is driven by innovation, for the purpose of driving the breakthrough and development of all fields. Such a strategy might encompass: growth impetus should be converted from investment orientation to innovation orientation, so as to form a new impetus mechanism; the economic form should be converted from the industrial economy to service economy, so as to establish an industrial structure in which the service sector plays the major part; industrial orientation should be converted from low-end to high-end, so as to gradually establish a new type of industrial system oriented by high end, intensification and service; city development should be converted from aggregation to the coexistence of aggregation and radiation, and the city should be completely integrated into the global city network by constantly improving the urban comprehensive service function and internationalization level; the urban form should be converted from mononuclear and monopole to multinuclear and multipole, so as to form the urban spatial layout of the metropolis; the economic development mode is converted from the extensive mode with high energy consumption to the green mode with low carbon emissions, so as to explore a new development path characterized by harmony between humans, nature and the environment; the focus on economic development of the city is switched to the harmonious development of the economy, society and culture, so as to vigorously promote cultural prosperity and comprehensively construct a harmonious society; the opening pattern is converted from opening up to the outside world to opening up to both the inside and outside world, so as to vigorously drive forward the integration of the Yangtze River Delta and promoting joint development.

2. Promoting the innovation of technology, finance, culture, urban form and administrative mode

Taking innovation orientation as the main thread, Shanghai will strive to promote technological innovation, with the focus shifted to secondary innovation and integrated innovation. The city will improve its capacity for independent innovation, turning itself into an innovation center of high and new technologies such as information, biotechnology, new energy and environmental protection. Shanghai will also promote financial innovation and make financial opening up and innovation a pilot project, building the key innovation base of financial products in Shanghai or even in the entire

Asia-Pacific region. Cultural innovation will be driven forward, to build 'China's fashion and creation culture metropolis'; the innovation of urban form will also be promoted, so as to create an urban form that matches the development of global cities; the innovation of urban administration will be promoted, in order to form an administrative mode of global cities that is both in line with international practice and suitable for a developing country.

3. Promoting the upgrading of economic transformation by relying on the 'four centers' and the pilot free trade zone

(1) Relying on the construction of 'four centers', Shanghai accelerates the development of a modern service industry and promotes the adjustment and upgrading of the industrial structure, with a focus on the listing of crude oil futures, the construction of a new online insurance ecommerce platform (Fangxin (Assured) insurance), and the agglomeration of functional financial agencies, propping up the development of internet finance and privately operated finance. High-end shipping services are to be developed, such as shipping finance, shipping insurance, maritime laws and the cruise economy. Pudong airport is being supported to expand the scale of cargo and mail transshipment, and the development of shipping derivatives are being promoted. A bulk commodity trading platform is being built and modern logistics is developed and optimized. The plan to accelerate commercial transformation and upgrade competitive power is put into practice to promote the integrated development of traditional commerce and ecommerce. The building of a world-famous tourist city is promoted, and service consumption is largely encouraged, such as information consumption, tourism consumption, health consumption and experience consumption, to motivate the development of producer and consumer services.

(2) Relying on the construction of the pilot free trade zone to promote system innovation and upgrade economic transformation, Shanghai strives to frame the basic system structure consistent with prevailing practices in international investment trade, which includes the further promotion of investment administration system reform, the innovation of the trade supervision system, the establishment of the freight classification supervision mode, and the promotion of the integration of domestic and foreign trade. Financial opening and innovation is deepened, and pilot reform is implemented in fields of cross-border use of the renminbi, renminbi capital account convertibility, interest rate liberalization and foreign exchange administration to promote the development of the real economy, with the premise being that risk is under control. The service industry is further opened

up, and all the opening measures made in the general plan are to be fulfilled to promote linkages between the pilot free trade zone and the 'four centers'. A series of systems is established to improve government transparency in service and administration, which include the basic system of supervision during and after the event, the safety examination mechanism, the anti-monopoly investigation mechanism, the enterprise annual report publicity system, credit management system, integrated law enforcement system, and the supervision information-sharing mechanism across departments. The intellectual property protection mechanism is established, which integrates patent, trademark and copyright administration.

IV. Constructing the main functional area and optimizing the spatial layout[4]

Under the unified deployment of the State Council, Shanghai takes the initiative to make a plan of the main functional area, which means that in accordance with the resource- and environment-carrying capabilities of different regions and the current development intensification and potential, Shanghai will make a unified plan about future population and economic distribution, land utilization and urbanization pattern, classifying the land space, defining the main functions, ascertaining the development direction, controlling the development intensity, normalizing the development order, perfecting the development policy, and gradually forming a spatial development pattern in which the population, resources, economy and environment are in great harmony.

1. Constructing the main functional area 'with clearer functional layout, gradually optimized spatial structure, highly efficient land use, gradually reduced regional gap, and constantly improved ecological environment'

Shanghai mainly lays emphasis on the adjustment and optimization of the spatial structure, reasonable control over the population size and the protection of the ecological environment. It fulfills the demonstration role of the key region, and drives forward the creation of a new spatial development pattern in which the whole urban functions are optimized, the region's main function is conspicuous, and economic society is in harmony with the population, resources and environment. Shanghai plans to promote the formation of main body functional areas in 2020, with the

---

[4] *Shanghai Planning of Main-body Functional Areas*

major targets being as follows. The functional layout is more distinct and the layout of population and economy is more balanced, with the expected permanent population in the whole city being about 26.5m, and the main body functions of various functional regions being more conspicuous. As a result, the spatial land development pattern, which conforms to the needs of the 'four centers' and the socialist modern metropolis, has been primarily formed. The spatial structure is gradually optimized, and strict control is practiced over the scale of new construction land. Land resources should be vitalized in an efficient manner, with the land-use structure further optimized, so that ecological safety and the minimum amount of agricultural inputs could be efficiently guaranteed. The efficiency of land use is being improved conspicuously, and in built-up areas, the population density and carrying capability of resources and the environment are becoming more harmonious. Land use is more intensive and economical, and land productivity is conspicuously boosted. The regional gap is gradually being reduced, as is the gap between different functional areas, in terms of the development level of economic society, the income of inhabitants, fundamental public services and the ecological environment. A new pattern of urban and rural integration development has already been formed, with the balance and coordination of the development in the whole city being further reinforced. The ecological environment has been constantly improved and the stability of the ecological system has been enhanced, so that the environmental quality is greatly improved, with the total emission of pollutants constantly being reduced and the defenses against natural disasters being constantly improved.

2. Division of the urban space into four functional areas

In accordance with the requirements of the *National Planning of Main Functional Areas*, and in combination with the actual situation in Shanghai, land in the city is divided into four types of functional area in addition to the sporadically distributed areas that are prohibited from being developed and those that are allowed to be developed but with many restrictions.

(1) The urban function optimization area mainly covers central urban districts such as Huangpu, Xuhui and Changning, and combined urban-rural districts such as Baoshan and Minhang. These areas have a lot of urban charm as a result of their culture and history. They are the main carriers representing innovative vitality and an emerging service industry, and are modern international areas with an agglomeration of high-end factors.

(2) The new area of metropolitan development, limited to Pudong new district. This area needs to optimize the population structure and layout, and to promote a new round of regional functional development, so as to coordinate urban and rural integration. It is essential that this area should vigorously improve global resource allocation capacity and further deepen reform and opening up, so as to lead the transformation of the whole city. The regional orientation of this area is the core functional area of the 'four centers', the dominating area of strategic emerging industries and the demonstration area of national reform.

(3) The new-type urbanization area includes suburban areas such as Jiading and Jinshan districts. The urban construction of such areas has benefited from previous economic development, with great potential for future development. However, there is an ever-growing conflict between the rapid growth of the permanent population and the lagging behind of the functions of new towns, and thus public services and the resource environment are under great pressure. Therefore, the functional orientation of such areas is both the base of advanced manufacturing industry and of key strategic emerging industries, which has upgraded global competitiveness. Such areas are also the main carriers unifying the regional harmonious development of urban and suburban areas, sustaining the strategic space and new growth pole in which innovation drives development and economic transformation is upgraded.

(4) The integrated ecological development area, comprising Chongming county. This is the experimental area of national sustainable development, and a modernized integrated ecological island. It is an important strategic part of Shanghai's sustainable development, and it requires further ecological construction and environmental protection. The population needs to be distributed in a reasonable way, and linkages between the three islands of Chongming need to be promoted so as to enhance sustainable development capability.

(5) The area where development is allowed but with some restrictions mainly refers to places with a high ecological conservation and agricultural ecology value. Here, restrictions need to be imposed on large-scale and highly intensified industrial and urban development.

(6) The area prohibited from development mainly refers to the various natural resource protection areas that are established by law, and some areas requiring special protection. Such areas are of paramount importance for the maintenance of urban ecological safety, and therefore industrial and urban development is prohibited.

3. Further optimizing the spatial layout

On the basis of the current spatial situation, Shanghai will vigorously construct an urban pattern of 'two axes and two belts, multilayer and multinuclear models', promoting the optimization of the urban spatial layout. One of the two axes runs east to west, alongside Hongqiao business district, Hongqiao ETDZ and up to Zhangjiang Hi-tech Park, the international tourist holiday zone and the Pudong airport area, building an urban development axis characterized by the typical cityscape of an international metropolis and the functions of 'four centers'. The other axis runs north to south, along the Huangpu river through the districts of Yangpu, Xuhui and Minhang, building the Huangpu river development axis that reflects the urban historical culture and international high-end service functions. The two belts are the east development belt along the coast and riverside, and the west development belt along the Huning and Huhang expressways. The multinuclear model refers to improving the comprehensive service functions and the internationalization of the central city, and promoting the development of new town clusters in the west and new towns along the riverside and coastline. Shanghai will also construct a fundamental ecological network pattern of 'circle, corridor, district and origin', forming a fundamental ecological pattern with multilayers, networks and compound functions, improving the quality of the urban ecological environment and improving the quality of the ecological environment for inhabitants.

V. Fostering and developing strategic emerging industries

Shanghai will vigorously promote the innovation and agglomeration of strategic emerging industries, accelerating the construction of a new type of industrial system that takes the modern service industry as the majority, strategic emerging industry as the bellwether and advanced manufacturing industry as the support, so as to constantly improve industrial core competitiveness.[5]

1. Sticking to market orientation, the enterprise as the main body, impetus by innovation, priority breakthrough and the importance of development and training

Shanghai will stick to market orientation, combining the decisive role exerted by the market in resource allocation and the guiding role played by the

---

[5] The Twelfth Five-year Plan of Shanghai Strategic Emerging Industry Development, 2012

government; stick to enterprises as the main body, making sure that enterprises grow to become the main investors, main researchers and practitioners of the achievements of strategic emerging industries; stick to impetus by innovation, vigorously promoting original innovation, reinforcing integrated innovation and re-innovation after introduction and absorption, mastering a batch of core technologies and related property rights; stick to priority breakthrough, combining the integral advancement and leapfrogging development of some key fields; stick to the importance of development and training, combining the promotion of sustainable development and the support of current development, and attaching importance to long-term development.

2. Exerting the key driving force of strategic emerging industries

Shanghai fosters and develops strategic emerging industries for the purpose of making them the key driving force of Shanghai's economy and social development, and leading the optimization and upgrading of the industrial structure. Targets include building the agglomeration of strategic emerging industries that lead the country in comprehensive strength and top the world in some fields; building a government service system that is comprehensive, multilayered and efficient, forming a favorable service environment propping up the development of strategic emerging industries; forming a pattern in which innovative factors are active and innovative capabilities are outstanding, and the achievements can be promptly applied with industrial features being distinct.

3. Focusing on the five leading industries and two forerunner industries

To develop strategic emerging industries, Shanghai will lay stress upon five leading industries: new-generation information technology, high-end equipment manufacturing, biotechnology, new energy and new materials. New-generation information technology includes integrated circuits, communications and networks, new-type displays, automotive electronics, software and information services. In high-end equipment manufacturing, emphasis will be put on raising the capabilities of independent design, manufacturing and advanced major equipment, so as to develop intelligent manufacturing equipment with the core being digitization, flexibility and system integration techniques, and to accelerate the development of clean and efficient coal power equipment, gas turbines, railway transportation equipment, key basic parts, testing equipment and ocean

Chapter 7

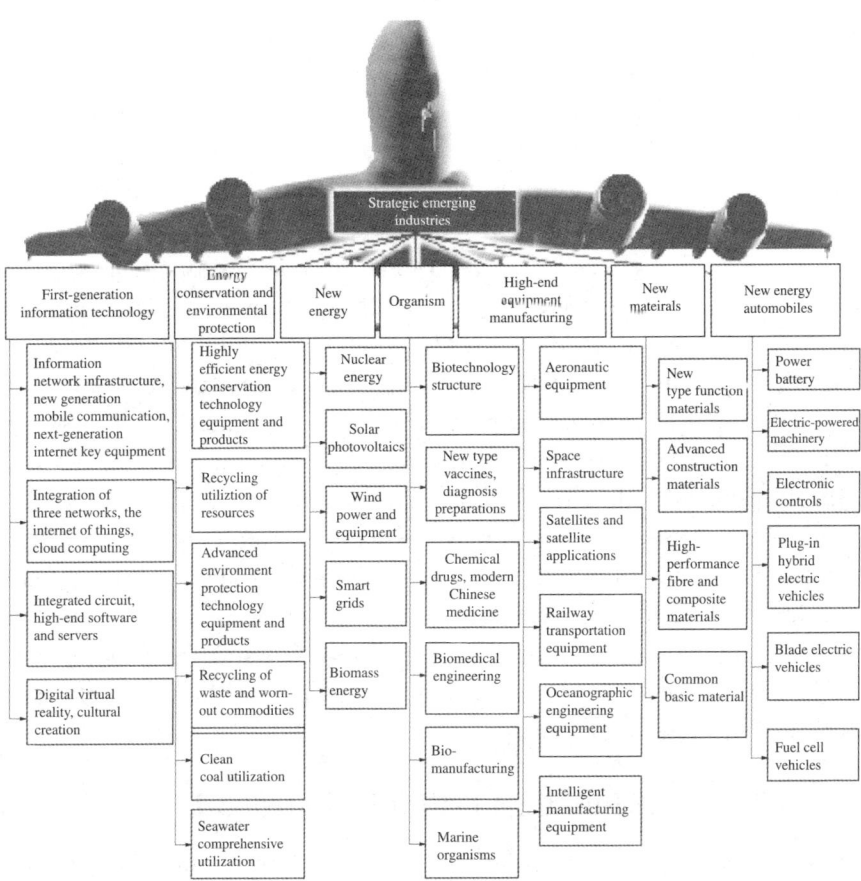

Figure 7-1 The development focuses of Shanghai's strategic emerging industries[6]

---

[6] Cited from stock.tzt.cn

engineering equipment. The biotechnology industry will center on key technological innovation and industrialization, with a focus on the fields of biological medicine and medical apparatus and instruments, so as to bring about leapfrog development. The new materials industry will exert the advantages of leading enterprises in technology and scale, to foster emerging enterprises with innovative vitality. With an eye on key new materials that are dependent on the development of strategic emerging industries, key technologies and industrialization should be deployed to overcome difficulties, with an effort to raise the share of key new material products that have high added value and small impact on the environment, and sustain the development of strategic emerging industries. Shanghai will also foster the energy conservation and environment protection industries, as well as new-energy automobiles. Energy conservation and environmental protection will tackle key core technologies such as the efficient employment of energy, recycling and the prevention of pollution, with emphasis on the development of new equipment and products that are energy-efficient, environmentally friendly and cyclic in resource utilization, so as to develop service industries in energy conservation and environmental protection. The new energy automobile industry will give priority to the development of plug-in hybrid electric vehicles, blade electric vehicles and pure electric buses with battery capacitors, continuing research and development into fuel cell vehicles and striving to make breakthroughs in the key core technologies of 'electric batteries, electrical machines and electronic control'.

VI. Building a cultural metropolis

Since the opening of its port, at the intersection of Chinese and western civilizations and the integration of ancient and modern cultures, Shanghai has formed a distinct and vibrant culture that draws on its own traditions and foreign influences. The present era has raised new requirements with regard to its cultural construction, for this is an era in which opening up is being expanded and information channels dramatically increased, with more diversified social ideological trends and public thinking. Shanghai is taking the initiative to undertake a major national cultural strategic task, striving to expand cultural exchange and cooperation both at home and abroad, consciously and actively promoting the construction of a cultural metropolis, and establishing a spiritual home that is shared by all its citizens.

1. Propelling the construction of a socialist core value system

Shanghai will reinforce the guiding role of the socialist core value system and promote a national spirit centered on patriotism and the current era, centered on reform and innovation, and establish and practice the socialist concept of honor and disgrace, ensuring a common ethical basis shared by all civilians. The city spirit of 'absorbing and accommodating, committed to excellence, enlightened and farsighted, modest and generous' will be vigorously promoted and fostered, and enriched in practice so as to be integrated into every aspect of city life, and to be converted into a powerful impetus driving the city's development. Spiritually civilized activities will be universally carried out for the purpose of guiding civilians in the development of civilized lifestyles and the sharing of a beautiful life. The establishment of a learning society will be further promoted, for learning enhances moral fiber, accumulates wisdom, and helps start businesses, and thus an ideal situation will be formed, in which everyone is willing to learn, anytime and anywhere.

2. Improving the creation and production of spiritual cultural products

Shanghai will propel the innovative development of philosophy and social science, improve the capability and level of theoretical innovation, academic research, social services and cultural inheritance, and build a key position in the academic field in which philosophy and social science can prosper. Shanghai will also build a key base of original literary work, leading the correct direction of literary creation and reinforcing the creation of 'novel works, excellent works and quality works'. Another measure is to enhance international cultural exchange and cooperation and promote learning from each other, so that the international influence and radiation of Shanghai culture is reinforced, with the carriers being Shanghai Week, international partnership cities, partnership communities and Shanghai city image ambassador.

3. Building a national top-notch public cultural service system

Shanghai will build sound public cultural service facilities and construct a sound public cultural service facility system at different levels of the city, district, sub-district and neighborhood, in accordance with the requirements of a balanced layout, integrated functions and convenient services. The effective supply of public cultural products and services must be guaranteed, and more public cultural venues should be open to the public free of charge, such as cultural centers, museums, libraries, art galleries and memorial museums. Schools, gymnasiums and stadiums, enterprises and institutions are encouraged to open their facilities to the public. Mass cultural activities are vigorously carried out, and it is advocated that everyone participates and enjoys doing so. The masses are encouraged to create and perform by themselves, and to conduct various kinds of cultural activities based on their local conditions. A public cultural service system and mechanism shall be innovated, and planning, coordination, service and guarantee shall be reinforced, and the unified management of public cultural construction and administration at district and county levels shall be enhanced. The protection, inheritance and administration of cultural relics should be strengthened, along with the administration of cultural relic preservation institutions and immovable cultural relics, so that local modern cultural relics of historic, artistic and scientific value are well protected.

4. Promoting cultural creation as a pillar industry

The layout of the cultural creation industry should be optimized in such a way that a cultural creation industry axis, industry belt and industry circle can be formed in Shanghai. Shanghai will foster and assist the main body of the cultural market, and stimulate the further opening of the cultural market, encouraging and guiding the sound development of cultural enterprises under various types of ownership, so as to form a creation industry development pattern that is oriented by public ownership with joint development of various systems of ownership. The industrial development environment should be improved to stimulate cultural property rights transactions, the international cultural service trade and the establishment of a cultural creation industry with generic technology services and cultural intermediary services. To promote the 'going global' of cultural products and services, Shanghai is accelerating the development of cultural creation service trade, and expanding the trade of cultural creation products and services, on the basis of the construction of Shanghai's capacity as an international trade center.

5. Building exceptional cultural talent

The team of cultural talent should be strengthened, and a series of key talent development plans should be put into effect, such as a cultural master funding plan, a leading talent developing plan, a young talent training plan and an overseas talent introduction plan, attracting and fostering leading talent both at home and abroad. Cultural talent should be encouraged to improve their qualities and bear social responsibility, acting as role models of moral character and personal integrity. A policy favorable to attracting cultural talent should be perfected, with an emphasis on major projects and major bases. Such a favorable policy may also cover expanding the platform establishment of starting a business, establishing a cultural talent development fund, guaranteeing designated investment in cultural talent projects, fostering an environment favorable to cultural creation, and providing the development space for cultural talent.

VII. Building a world-famous tourist city

It is clearly stated in *On Accelerating Tourism Development and Constructing a World-famous Tourist City (2011)* issued by Shanghai Municipal Party Committee of the CPC, that Shanghai will "strive to build 'a world-famous tourist city', and promote tourism to be a new strategic pillar industry and modern service industry".

1. Building 'five tourist destinations'

In terms of promoting the construction of a world-famous tourist city, Shanghai will build 'five tourist destinations' to cover the following: an international urban sightseeing destination that is highly attractive and highly reputed, and clustered with world-level scenery; an international urban fashion shopping destination that is equipped with convenient payment systems, a favorable environment, and agglomeration of international and national brands of commodities; an international urban commercial convention and exhibition destination that provides sound facilities, great services and conspicuous brand competitiveness; an international urban cultural tourist destination that integrates heritage and creativity, and gathers various festival celebrations and competitions; an international urban leisure holiday destination with a beautiful environment, rich connotations and unique charms, and thus is built into a tourist distribution center that provides convenient transfer stations, smooth connections and fast transportation transfer.

2. Forming a new tourism development pattern of 'one circle, four areas, three belts and one island'

(1) The 'one circle' refers to the central circle of urban tourism integrating commercial conventions and exhibitions, urban sightseeing, food and shopping, leisure and recreation, and cultural creativity.

(2) The 'four areas' refer to the eastern, western, southern and northern areas of Shanghai city. The eastern area contains theme parks, and conventions

and exhibitions, with a focus on building international tourist holiday resorts centered on Disneyland, commercial conventions and exhibitions tourism in Lingang New City, and ecological leisure holiday resorts along the coast. The western area is the scenic tourism and leisure holiday resort area, represented by distinctive leisure holiday resorts such as Sheshan and Dianshan Lake, thereby expanding the functional space of Shanghai as a world-famous tourist city. The southern area is a rural holiday and coastal recreation tourist area, with a focus on building the north bank of Hangzhou Bay as a distinctive coastal tourist area, while the rural holiday area includes Fengjing and Zhuanghang tourist areas. The northern area is an ecological leisure tourist area and industrial experience tourist area, with importance attached to ecological tourism and leisure holiday to form a new and expanded area of urban tourism in Shanghai.

(3) The 'three belts' cover the Huangpu river tourist belt of 'three riverside areas and 10 scenic spots', with the 'three riverside areas' referring to building greenery along the river, providing congestion-free transportation along the river and agglomerating tourist functions along the river. The '10 scenic spots' include Wusong watergate, Jiangwan Tower reflection and Maple island. Suzhou river townscape is another tourist belt, which fully takes advantage of the touring resources on and along the Suzhou river, attaching importance to the connection between water and land, and to resource integration, so as to develop a whole plan of high-quality water tourist commodities. The last belt is the coastal tourist belt on the north bank of Hangzhou Bay, which makes full use of coastal resources to promote the linkage between water and land, with Pudong Coastal Forest Park, Fengxian Bay tourist holiday resort and Jinshan coastal leisure holiday tourist resort being the priorities to build three water tourist belts on the Huangpu river, Suzhou river and the north bank of Hangzhou Bay.

(4) The 'one island' refers to the international ecological tourist island, which is meant to build the three islands in Chongming into a world-famous ecological island and rural sightseeing area, with Chenjia town, Dongping Forest Park and Pearl Lake being the focus of development.

3. Promoting the innovative development of the tourism type and service

To promote the construction of a world-famous tourist city, Shanghai will vigorously support innovation and the integrated development of tourism, and develop a tourism information service industry mainly represented by tourism ecommerce, virtual tourism, and travel planning and consultation. Shanghai will take advantage of its status as a manufacturing base to develop tourism manufacturing, such as the manufacturing of cruisers, pleasure boats, yachts, limousines, large recreation facilities and tour guide facilities. Shanghai reinforces the innovation of tourism finance, including encouraging financial agencies to diversity tourism credit service products and developing installment, guarantee and trusteeship. Shanghai further enhances the travel service functions of bank cards, vigorously promoting financial services such as travel credit cards, travelers' checks and travel financial management.

Chapter Follow-up Questions and References

Chapter 1

Questions:

1. What are the main factors driving forward the development of Shanghai?
2. Compared with other international metropolises such as London and New York, what are Shanghai's strong and weak points?
3. Compared with your city, what are the experiences and lessons that might be learnt from Shanghai?

References:

1. Shanghai Municipal Government, *The 12th Five-year Plan of Shanghai National Economy and Social Development [R]*, 2011
2. Zhou Zhenhua, et al, *Shanghai: City Evolution and Expectation [M]*. Shanghai: Truth and Wisdom Press, 2010
3. Xu Jiangang, et al, *The Thirty Years of Shanghai's Reform and Opening Up [M]*. Shanghai: Shanghai People's Publishing House, 2008
4. Qian Yunchun, Guo Linlin, *The Path of Pudong – Reflections and Future Prospects of 20 Years of Innovative Development [M]*. Shanghai: Shanghai People's Publishing House, 2010

Chapter 2

Questions:

1. What are the main contents of Shanghai's construction of 'four centers'?
2. What are the reasons for Shanghai's great economic achievements since reform and opening up?
3. Please illustrate how to apply Shanghai's practice of industrial restructuring to the practice in your country.

References:

1. Zuo Xuejin, et al, *Shanghai's Economic Reform and City Development: Practice and Experience* [M], Shanghai: Shanghai Academy of Social Sciences Press, 2008
2. You Jianxin, et al, 'Pattern Analysis of Innovative City Construction – with Shanghai and Shenzhen as Examples' [J], *China Soft Science*, 2011(7)
3. Zhou Zhenhua ed. *Innovation as the Impetus, and Development by Transformation: 2010-2011 Shanghai Development Report.* Shanghai: Truth and Wisdom Press and Shanghai People's Publishing House, 2011
4. Yuan Enzhen, et al, *Thirty Years of Shanghai: Reform and Opening Up and Economic Development* [M], Shanghai: Shanghai University of Finance and Economics Press, 2008

Chapter 3

Questions:

1. What are the fundamental experiences of community construction in Shanghai?
2. What are the main features of Shanghai's social security system?
3. How does Shanghai develop and improve social undertakings?

References:

1. Shanghai Municipal Government, *The 12th Five-year Plan of Shanghai's National Economy and Social Development* [R], 2011
2. Zhou Zhenhua, et al, *Shanghai: City Evolution and Expectation* [M]. Shanghai: Truth and Wisdom Press, 2010
3. Xu Jiangang, et al, *Thirty Years of Shanghai's Reform and Opening Up* [M]. Shanghai: Shanghai People's Publishing House, 2008
4. Qian Yunchun, Guo Linlin, *The Path of Pudong – Reflections and Future Prospects of Twenty Years of Innovative Development* [M]. Shanghai: Shanghai People's Publishing House, 2010

Chapter 4

Questions:

1. How does Shanghai carry out cultural system reform? And how is it different to your country or region?

2. How does Shanghai develop the cultural creation industries? How might this inspire your country or region?
3. What are the strong and weak points of Shanghai's development of urban tourism?

References:

1. Ye Xin, et al, *Shanghai Culture Development Report* [M]. Beijing: Social Sciences Academic Press, 2006-2012
2. Xie Liping, et al, *30 Years of Shanghai Culture Construction*, Shanghai: Shanghai People's Publishing House, 2008
3. Lu Hanlong, et al, *Shanghai Society Development Report* [M]. Beijing: Social Sciences Academic Press, 2006-2012
4. Sun Fuqng, et al, *A Tale of Two Cities – Shanghai and New York Urban Culture*. Shanghai: Shanghai People's Publishing House, 2011
5. Shanghai Cultural Development Foundation Research Group, 'Industry: Engine of the Creativity Economy', *Trade Review of Shanghai's Creative Industry*, Shanghai: Shanghai Joint Publishing Co., 2006

Chapter 5

Questions:

1. How can the relationship between urban ecological environment protection and social economic development be coordinated?
2. What is the role of the government in the protection of the urban ecological environment? How can the ecological environment be protected?
3. How can the public participate in the protection of the urban ecological environment? What are the possible approaches?

References:

1. Shanghai Municipal Government, *The '12th Five-year Plan' of Shanghai Environment Protection* [R]. 2012
2. Shanghai Municipal Government, *The Urban Green Land System Planning of Shanghai City (2002-2020)* [R]. 2002
3. Shanghai Municipal Government, *The '12th Five-year Plan' of Shanghai City Afforestation* [R]. 2012
4. Shanghai Municipal Government, *The '12th Five-year Plan' of Shanghai New Energy Development* [R]. 2012
5. Zhang Xiaoguo, Suzhou River: *Limpidity Is Not a Dream (French Version)* [M], Shanghai: Shanghai People's Publishing House, 2011

Chapter 6

Questions:

1. What are the core elements of urban transportation administration?
2. How could food safety administration be improved?
3. What are the major difficulties in urban appearance management? And what measure should be taken to tackle the difficulties?

References:

1. Shanghai Municipal Planning and Land and Resources Administration, Shanghai Urban Planning and Design Research Institute, *Transition Shanghai, Planning and Strategy* [M], Shanghai: Tongji University Press, 2012
2. Editorial Committee of Shanghai City Construction and Administration, *Shanghai City Construction and Administration* [M], Shanghai: Shanghai Science and Technology Press, 2010
3. Huang Rong, *The Public Transport Priority (Exploration and Practice of Shanghai Urban Transport)* [M], Shanghai: Shanghai People's Publishing House, 2012
4. Tang Minhao, *Research Report on Food and Drug Safety and Supervision* [M], Beijing: Social Sciences Academic Press, 2012
5. Chen Qiuling: *Study of Shanghai Urban Safety* [M], Shanghai: Economy and Management Publishing House, 2011

Chapter 7

Questions:

1. What are the main features and building paths of global cities?
2. What is the realistic significance of urban cultural inheritance?
3. How could the attraction of urban tourism be enhanced?

References:

1. Zhou Zhenhua, *Shanghai Report: Shanghai Stepping Towards a Global City – Strategy and Action* [M]. Shanghai: Shanghai Century Publishing Group, 2012
2. Zhou Zhenhua, *The 'Post-World Expo' Development of Shanghai* [M]. Shanghai: Truth and Wisdom Press, Shanghai People's Publishing House, 2011

3. Zhou Zhenhua, et al, *Shanghai: City Evolution and Expectation* [M]. Shanghai: Truth and Wisdom Press, 2010
4. Shanghai Municipal Government, *The Twelfth Five-year Plan of Shanghai's Strategic Emerging Industry Development* [R], 2012
5. Shanghai Municipal Government, *Decisions on Accelerating the Tourism Development and Constructing a World-famous Tourist City* [R], 2011